James McCullogh's Book

James McCullogh's Book

A Glimpse into Life on the Colonial Frontier

John Stauffer & Calvin Bricker

The Conococheague Institute

Mercersburg, Pennsylvania

James McCullogh's Book
A Glimpse into Life on the Colonial Frontier
© 2015 The Conococheague Institute

Published in the United States of America by

The Conococheague Institute
12995 Bain Road
Mercersburg, PA 17236
Phone: (717) 328-3467
Fax: (717) 328-2800
info@cimlg.org
www.cimlg.org
www.cimlg.org/blog
www.facebook.com/conococheagueinstitute

Cover by Silverback Designs
Produced by Black Walnut Corner Book Ptoduction

ISBN 978-0-9907116-2-9

Table of Contents

Foreword

James McCullogh purchased a pocket-sized leather-bound day-book in 1745, presumably in Belfast, Northern Ireland, before he and his wife set sail for America. In the days that have passed from then until now, the diary and account book survived intact through many generations. As the current and temporary possessor of this treasure, I am happy to see its story told in *James McCullogh's Book: A Glimpse into Life on the Colonial Frontier.*

This is not the first time that the diary has been featured in a publicatio. For example, my father made a presentation on it for Franklin County's Kittochtinny Historical Society, and a chapter is devoted to James McCullogh in the book, *Irish Immigrants in the Land of Canaan: Letters and Memoirs from Colonial and Revolutionary America, 1675-1815,* written and edited by Kerby Miller, Arnold Schrier, Bruce D. Boling and David N. Doyle (2003). This is the first time, however, that an entire book examines the life, times and writings of James McCullogh.

The diary came to me from my late father, Charles J. Stoner who loved and learned history, especially Franklin County history. Neither he nor I are related to James McCullogh, but Marion Krebs of Mercersburg, Pennsylvania, was a direct descendent.

I remember as a child making a visit with my parents to Mr. and Mrs. Krebs at their house on Linden Avenue. This was in the late 1950s or early 1960s. Mr. Krebs got the diary out and showed it to my father who was particularly interested because of the early local history it held, and just being in touch with something so old and yet, so immediate. One entry mentioned sale of fabric to David Stoner, my great-great-great-great- grandfather's brother.

Because of my father's interest in the diary, Marion Krebs eventually gave it to him before he died in 1968.

My plan is to place the diary in a secure archive where it can be maintained and protected in perpetuity.

Paula Stoner Reed, PhD
October 2015

Introduction

On a spring day in 1745, a 25-year-old Irishman of Scottish descent purchased a leather-bound notebook in the port city of Belfast. He then booked passage in advance for himself and his wife Martha to the New World, a land he doubtless hoped would be free from the religious and economic stresses he was feeling at home. James McCullogh, who had already showed himself to be a skilled weaver and shrewd businessman, carefully recorded these expenses in his new book, then tucked it away for nine months before he jotted down the next entry on the eve of his departure for American shores.

A dedicated journalist, James McCullogh was not. Because of that, the challenges of studying McCullogh's curious book have been great, considering all of its mysteries and idiosyncrasies. It has, however, been well worth the effort, as this was a primary source, one man's notes and musings that disclosed much about what newcomers more than 250 years ago faced when establishing a new life on the American frontier in Southern Pennsylvania.

The colonial immigrants could not have imagined or anticipated the difficulties that they would face, no matter what steps they took in preparation. This was not naiveté on their part, although they might have had dreams of unlimited opportunity, farming on fertile land, financial rewards and, above all perhaps, freedom. All of these dreams were possible in some sense, but the life-and-death struggles along the way could not have been anticipated. At the Conococheague Institute, we have sought to analyze the diary in the context of the culture of the times and the culture of a Scots-Irish immigrant, both of which are difficult to visualize in the framework of the twenty-first century, even when standing on the very soil that James McCullogh trod in the mid-1700s. So much has changed.

McCullogh calls this 114 page, 5 ½-by-8 inch, leather-bound booklet "His Book" when he starts making entries. But it is difficult to categorize: Is it a diary? Ledger? Log? Notebook? It is a little of all of these. For this study it is called a diary, yet in many ways it does not fit the definition of a diary, as it is mostly lacking in ordinary daily entries.

McCullogh does not record the weather or his daily personal thoughts, or dwell on his family or friends, or say anything about holidays or meals—most of the things we would find most important in our own day-to-day lives. Matters of family are minimal. He does not refer to his wife at all after leaving Ireland, yet she must have been at his right hand performing house and farm chores and weaving linen.

Nor is this book arranged chronologically; entries of different dates are recorded on the same page. It is somewhat categorized by subject. McCullogh did not number the pages of the diary; where there are references to page numbers in this work, these numbers were applied by us (the companion volume to this book, the facsimile of the actual diary, uses these same numbers we have applied for clarity).

The very first entry reads, "This book was bought in Belfast April the 27 1745 by James McCulloch." On another page, there is an entry of the same date that reads, "Belfast April ye 27, 1745 R'd of James

McCulloch six pounds (nearly $2,000 in today's U.S. dollars) for his and his wife's passage Arthur (Burrow?)." In 1746 there were no entries, despite a couple of life events that most would have thought noteworthy: crossing the Atlantic and the birth of a child.

Written in the preceding entry as "McCulloch," James used at least eight different spellings for his last name in the diary, a phenomenon that wasn't uncommon in that time. And the colonial records adopted another spelling with an added "u," (McCullough), an adaptation that James did not ever use in his diary. The spelling chosen by the authors, McCullogh, was the one that James used most often in his diary.

He came ashore in New Castle, now in the state of Delaware, in 1746. There's no diary entry confirming that, however. By entering at Newcastle, he would have avoided the oath of abrogation (of Catholicism) and allegiance to the crown of England required at other entry points. After arriving in America his entries into the diary increase, beginning with the one reading "His Book 1747." As can be seen, he kept a detailed record of the planting and harvesting of his crops and sale of products from his farm. His book records many transactions and the terms for payments, along with payments to farm workers. And he keeps careful records of his varied linen production and sales. Interspersed among the pages are religious reflections (see chapter 8) and coded numerical encryptions (see chapter 10).

Soon after his arrival in the Conococheague region near Mercersburg, Pa., the frontier was caught in a reign of terror, the result of the French and Indian War. McCullogh's diary provided an interesting record of many of these Indian raids and their outcomes, recording deaths, injuries and captives (see chapter 6). His entries include not only attacks on local settler forts and homes in the Conococheague

The Various Spellings of "McCullogh"

From Diary page 1, James M^{C}Cullogh

Diary Page 2, James m^{C}Colog

Diary Page 4, James M^{C}Culock

Diary Page 20, using code for "James," then M^{C}Collogh

Diary Page 21, Sara m^{C}Cullogh

Diary Page 32, Sara m^{C}Cullogh

Diary Page 42, Archibald mcColock

Diary Page 113, JAMES mCColloch

James McCullogh spelled his and his family's last names in a variety of ways, something that was not uncommon during this time.

region, but also many of the attacks within a 30- to 50-mile radius. The news of attacks somehow could travel quickly over a rugged countyside that still had no established roads. These entries provide helpful documentation of the turmoil encountered on the frontier.

Colonial diaries such as these rarely survived the ensuing generations, and many people are responsible for shepherding this one along through the years into our hands today. When one looks at the cracked leather binding, worn corners, and browned pages one marvels that it has survived. It attests to the importance that his descendants placed on this journal.

Credit goes to the James McCullough family descendants who, for over two centuries, cared for this small leather bound pocket book. We believe that the diary passed from James' widow, Martha, to son John, to John II (d. 1882), to John III (d. 1910), to his daughter, Nancy Cannon McCollough Kreps and then to her son, Marion Kreps. In

order that the diary could be safeguarded by the historical community, Marion Krebs, gave it to Charles J. Stoner, a Mercersburg, Pa., artist and historian. The transcription of the diary was done by Dr. David Wallace of Frederick, Md.

While the diary was in his hands, Charles J. Stoner reviewed it and presented his interpretation to the Franklin County (Kittochinny) Historical Society on Feb. 24, 1984. He also provided copies of the diary pages to scholars, such as those who wrote the book *Irish Immigrants in the Land of Canaan*, published in 2003. Twenty-two pages of Chapter 21 are devoted to the McCullogh diary, from 1748 to 1758. Their works greatly aided the interpretation found in this work.

The McCullogh diary has been brought to our attention several times over the past 50 years, but there was so much more to its pages that we at the Conococheague Institute took on the task of a more thorough examination of its contents. Numerous individuals of the Conococheague Institute who have studied it in recent years have made contributions to this present interpretation, from genealogical research, historical research, reading and advising on various sections, proofreading and editing. Among those contributing were Ann Allen, Martha Stauffer, Leda Werner, James Houpt and Gay Buchanan, to name a few.

Paula Stoner Reed, a life-long preservationist, made this work possible by providing full access to this historic and fragile journal. As custodian for this booklet, she kindly brought it from the safekeeping storage vault so that each page could be carefully photographed. Mercersburg Printing produced the images and archived them in digital form to allow a better chance of interpretation of pages that are difficult to read. Photographs of the journal pages are included in the aforementioned companion volume to this book, with a transcription of each page. Even after rereading of the original pages, we have had difficulty in making accurate transcriptions of some pages as we have difficulty reading some of the script. Some of the writing has faded and some of the pages have been overwritten, that is, written on the same page at some later date. We have done out best to quote his entries accurately, but some words unavoidably represent educated guesses.

Still, given the paucity of colonial diaries that have survived, Mc-Cullogh's work is priceless. Colonial diaries, log books or ledgers are a treasure for their personal insight into the times. Most of these American diaries were written by well-educated and prosperous inhabitants in the populated areas along the East Coast. One example is the existing diary written by Virginia planter William Bryd II, who bared his many sins for the later world to see. Like McCullogh, Byrd was known to write in code; unlike McCullogh he wrote freely about abuse of his slaves and family, and his "wicked thoughts" about the wenches, all of which he regretted until he did it the next time.

Mary Rowlandson, the wife of a Massachusetts preacher, wrote a narrative of her experiences with the Native Americans after she and her three children were captured during King Philip's War in 1675. Some kept journals for specific purposes, including botanist John Bartram, the Quaker abolitionist preacher John Woolman and Elizabeth Drinker, who kept a diary from 1738 to the Revolution. Our Founding Fathers shared a lot of their thoughts through their letters and diaries—Benjamin Franklin, John Adams, Thomas Jefferson—these were all learned men.

Even though there is no record of George Washington having a high school or college-styled education, he had commendable writing skills and kept almost daily entries during most of his adult years. It was not a simple process to keep a diary such as George Washington did, especially when on the road. When traveling from place to place on horseback, he had to carry the supplies in his saddlebag. To write entries, he took dried ink powder and added water to make it the right consistency for legible writing. He had to carry a penknife to sharpen the point of his quill pen, and he had to carry drying powder to absorb the moisture from the ink so that the script would not smear. The light available to him might have only been from a fireplace, a candle or torch.

In contrast to those colonial icons, James McCullogh was not a man of letters. Scots in general seemed to emphasize education, but from what we see in McCullogh's writing, it appears he did not have a high level of schooling, using phonetic spelling often and variations in spelling (not unusual in colonial times). However, he would have had more education than most of the other settlers on the frontier. It was rare for a pioneer to keep a diary—but not unknown. Frontier minister Charles Beatty kept a journal from 1762 to 1769, as he was supporting the great migration of Scots-Irish to the American frontier that brought thousands of Presbyterians to the wilderness.

Allen Brown, an immigrant from County Tyrone, Ireland, to the West Conococheague region, kept a frontier ledger following the French and Indian War. Brown arrived about 1755 and built a house on Forbes Road, the main road leading to Pittsburgh. He traded with soldiers, Indians and settlers, keeping a ledger of receipts and sales from 1764 to 1770, covering the years after Pontiac's War. Remaining in the Conococheague area his entire life, he is buried in the White Church Presbyterian graveyard. His ledger is privately owned and has never been published, although some of its content was made available by an auction house that sold it in 2008 (purchaser unknown). One entry notes the purchase of wheat, salt and whiskey in Carlisle, presumably supplies for him to sell. Another entry was an account of goods sold to British forces: "Moheare" at Fort Pitt and "Flanel" for local brigades.

Three frontier women who had been kidnapped by Indians wrote of their captivity—diaries collectively known as "captivity records"—even though women were generally afforded inferior educations. Those who were captured and wrote about it included Mary Draper Ingles, whose New River settlement home is near present-day Radford, Va., and Jean McCord Lowry, who was taken from the Conococheague settlement near to James McCullogh's farm. Mary Jemison's captivity began in the Buchanan Valley west of Gettysburg, from where she was marched westward over mountains and valleys crossing the west branch of the Conococheague Creek in Path Valley. These diaries have all been published (see the Bibliography), with that of Mary Draper Ingles written by her son John from what his mother shared. The diary of Jean McCord Lowry is discussed on page 69.

Col. James Smith, who is best known for leading the Black Boys Rebellion—a nine-month uprising against British failures to keep weapons and rum out of Indian hands—kept a diary during his years as a captive of the Indians from 1755 to 1759, later published as *An Account of the Remarkable Occurrences in the Life and Travels of Col. James Smith, during his captivity with the Indians*, published in 1799. More on Col. James Smith is covered in chapter 6.

McCullogh's own two sons were captured by the Indians in 1756, with the elder son John eventually publishing an account of his eight years in captivity. The younger son, James, was never heard from again. Such were the vagaries of the frontier of colonial America, and it's part of what makes the study of these diaries so fascinating.

This work will explore James McCullogh's so-named "His Book" in detail and refer to some of the other diarists to flesh out the story of the pioneers who journeyed into the unknown not once but twice, crossing the Atlantic and then boring into the unknown interior of what to them would have been a foreign nation in every sense of the term. Their determination comes through in the pages of his book, as the McCullogh family clawed its way to success and built a foundation for future generations of Americans to realize their own dreams. When we look at all the advantages we as a nation enjoy today, his book reminds us that we all in some sense are standing on the shoulders of people like James McCullogh.

CHAPTER 1

The Forces Behind Scots-Irish Migration

In the time of James McCullogh and his ancestors, neither Scotland nor the British Isles as a whole were peaceful places. Wars ravaged the countryside, clans were at each other's throats and rulers were executed with such regularity that it's hard to see how the job was in any way desirable. As violent at the colonial frontier might later prove to be, it certainly would have been no more bloody that the state of perpetual conflict that faced the Scots in their native country. When they weren't fighting each other, they were fighting for a bite to eat or the right to worship as they saw fit. The climate was changing and crops weren't dependable for the poor, lowland residents of Scotland. Nor could they count on being left alone in the practice of their new Presbyterian religion, which in one form or another was burning its way across Europe and promising even more in the way of conflict and persecution. Seeking peace, economic stability and religious freedom, thousands of Scots would move from their homes to the nearby country of Ireland to begin a new life. A century later, still searching for the same three things, they would move all over again.

The Scottish McCullogh clan warred with other clans in Scotland in the fifteenth and sixteenth century before moving to Northern Ire-

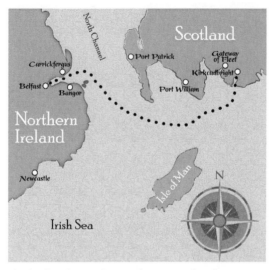

The broken line indicates the route taken by many in the steady stream of Scots from southern Scotland to Northern Ireland during the 1600s and early 1700s.

land in the seventeenth. The origin of the surname is told in the Book of Ulster Surnames by Robert Bell. The Ulster Gaelic names Mac Cu' Uladh or Mac Con Uladh both mean the "son of the hound of Ulster." This seems to have come from the Scots Gaelic, Mac Cullaich dating from 1296, when Thomas Maculagh rendered homage to Edward I. In the fifteenth century, this family held castles in the southern Scottish lowlands, one at Gatehouse of Fleet in Kurcudbrightshir, Cardoness Castle. In Scotland the McCulloghs were not a dominant clan and needed to be allied with larger clans as McDougalls, Rosses, and Monroes. McCulloghs were involved in many conflicts. One was a raid by Alexander McCullogh in 1530 on the Island of Man, south of the Scottish lowlands in the Irish Sea between England and Ireland, in retaliation for a raid by the Isle's resident Manx on Scottish Galloway.

James McCullogh's odyssey could be said to have been set in motion by King James VI, the colorful son of Mary Queen of Scots, who later become known as James I when he unified the Scottish and English crowns. Aside from having a Bible named after him, the popular King James ruled over an era of relative peace. He was a literary scholar and patron of the arts, but enlightened as he might have appeared, he was nevertheless terrified of witches and provided ample background material for Shakespeare's Macbeth.

His role in the McCullogh story has to do with his policy known as the Plantation of Ulster, the colonization of Northern Ireland by Scots and English in the early 1600s. James hoped that Scottish and English people and their laws could civilize a troublesome, nomadic native population that was prone to rebellion, so they were encouraged to move onto lands previously owned by Irish nobility. Irish rebels had long been at war with the English establishment, ultimately losing in a conflict known as the Nine Years War.

While James was not particularly vindictive, the Gaelic chiefs after the war enjoyed fewer economic privileges. As a response, about 90 Irish landholders sailed from Ireland to mainland Europe, hoping to stir up trouble between the Spanish and English in the Sept. 14, 1607, "Flight of the Earls." It was poor timing, however, because the Spanish navy had just been wiped out by the Dutch in the Battle of Gibraltar, and Spain was more interested in peace than rekindling hostilities with England. Following the Flight of the Earls, England confiscated their lands and called upon McCullogh's people to step in and fill the void.

Members of the McCullogh clan were among these Presbyterians who left the Scottish lowlands during the plantation period to find a new life in Northern Ireland. In the counties of Londonderry and

Down, the land could be used to raise sheep or grow flax, which were the life blood of Scottish weavers. These new immigrants leased land from plantation owners such as Sir George Rawdon, and thrived on the trade in wool and linen. James McCullogh farmed near the Town of Ballyhinch in County Downs on the eastern side of Ulster, not far west across the straight that separates Ireland from Scotland. Ballyhinch lies 15 miles north of Newcastle, Ireland, and about the same distance south of Belfast.

During the 1600s and early 1700s, a steady stream of Scots crossed from southern Scotland to Northern Ireland. Many took the route called the "Sheuch" from Wigtonshie to County Down in Ireland (see the broken line on the map). In Petty's census of 1659, Mac Cullogh was listed as one of the principle names in the Irish Baronies of Antrim, Belfast, Carrickfergus, Toome, and the Iveagh in County Down. The migration trade was at first dominated by Hugh Montgomery, a soldier and aristocrat known as a Founding Father of the Ulster Scots, who renamed Port Patrick as Port Montgomery. In our research, without knowing James McCullogh's ancestry, it has not been possible to ascertain the exact location when his ancestors settled in Northern Ireland or exactly where James grew up and was introduced to the flax and linen business. With "John" showing up regularly in his family, it is suspected that he had a father or uncle John. We know there was a John McCullogh born in 1686.

The lowland Scots, mainly artisans, weavers and laborers on the bottom rungs of the economic ladder, were willing to move to Ireland to escape economic travails, violence and religious persecution. Instead, through the course of the next century, they found more of the same. When John Knox brought Martin Luther's Reformation movement to Scotland, the resulting Presbyterian Church (one governed by elected representatives rather than a single bishop) was subjected to persecution by the state church. It was no different in Ireland. Presbyterian ministers were required to swear an oath to the Church of Ireland prayer book, which they seldom did, meaning that they could be deposed of their ministries. Weddings and funerals by law also had to conform to the rites of the state church, or they were considered to be invalid—meaning, among other things, that couples married in the Presbyterian church were not legally married at all and could theoretically be hauled up on charges of immoral behavior.

The same restrictions were in effect in other English colonies. For example, in the 1730s, Rev. William Williams, a Presbyterian minister, went as a missionary to the Shenandoah Valley of Virginia, taking with him his three surviving daughters after his wife and eight other children died. While in Virginia, he violated the restrictions of the Anglican Church by performing a marriage ceremony. He was jailed but fled on pretrial release to Maryland. He bought land on the Monocacy and then at Prices Ford on the Conococheague near Welsh Run.

Because of this, many marriage ceremonies were performed in secret, without being recorded—which explains the difficulty in tracking the McCullogh family history.

Ireland would not prove to be more peaceful than Scotland. English policies of populating Ulster with Scots naturally did not sit well with the native population. On a Friday night in the autumn of 1641, the Old-Irish landholder Sir Phelim O'Neill walked into the Castle Charlemont on the pretext of searching for stolen cattle and quickly secured its surrender. By the end of the weekend he held a string of forts and assuming he had the upper hand, announced a relatively tame set of administrative demands. His cohorts, however, who were supposed to secure the powerful Dublin Castle were betrayed and captured. From there, what started out as a limited action for the political rights of Irish gentry spun into 11 years of open warfare. The English overreacted with a brutal assault on Irish Catholic countrymen who, in turn, were inspired to join the Irish conspirators and took out their own brand of vengeance on the Ulster Scots, even though it had initially been agreed that the Scots were to have been left alone. Instead, Ulster planters were massacred by the thousands, and thousands more were driven from their homes, where they died of exposure.

For several more months, both sides committed atrocities against civilians before the war became more orderly, in a sense, fought by traditionally raised armies rather than torch-wielding mobs. It went on like this until one and all were overrun by the forces of Oliver Cromwell, who brought things full circle in 1653 by executing Phelim O'Neill.

To some extent the Irish Confederate Wars, as they were collectively known, were touched off and fed by growing economic trouble, as the Little Ice Age played havoc with European crops. In this respect, the hand of nature was aided and abetted by the hand of man. The arrival of French Huguenots in the 1680s strengthened the Ulster textile industry by introducing some new methods for the manufacture of linen from flax. But in the 1690s, the English parliament began to impose trade restrictions on the manufacture and trade of wool and linen. The Woolens Act of 1699 prohibited the exportation of Irish wool and linen to anywhere except England and Wales, creating an economic depression in Ulster. Then in the early 1700s, the plantation owners started a practice of rack-renting, by which they raised rents when the lease ran out, quite a departure from the traditional practice in the 1600s when leases were renewed at the same rate.

Taken together, these difficulties proved to be too much; many families resolved to leave. It is noteworthy that these three issues—religion, business, violence—were the three dominant themes in McCullogh's book. They were clearly sensitive topics that had an institutional memory all their own. For the Ulster Presbyterians, the final straw might have been the period from 1714 to 1719, when a severe drought added to the hardship by hindering the growth of food crops and flax. A flood of migration to American began in 1717 and continued to 1775, with Pennsylvania generally chosen for their destination in the New World. The McCulloghs would be among the estimated 200,000 to 250,000 Ulster Presbyterians who would pack up and board a ship for the British colonies.

These Ulster Presbyterians became known as "Scotch-Irish," a term that initially at least was something of a slur. Court testimony in the late 1600s questioned how it could be considered a sin to kill "any Scotch-Irish dogg." This fits a fairly constant pattern in history—the new minority on the block is disrespected. A half-century later, it would be the turn of the Irish to arrive on American shores, driven by starvation resulting from the potato famine of the mid 1800s, to become everyone's favorite whipping boy. At that time, the Ulster decedents embraced the term "Scotch-Irish" to differentiate themselves from Irish ne'er-do-wells. Nowadays, however, most agree that "Scots-Irish" is the preferred term and is what will be used in this book.

The men and women who were preparing to embark on a journey to the new world would wind up playing no small role in the destiny of America. The Scots-Irish were industrious, evangelical and seemingly had a bone to pick with anyone trying to govern them. In a historical retrospective, the Irish Times noted that these peoples "played a role (in the American Revolution) all out of proportion to their numbers." One British officer agreed, grumbling, "Call this war by whatever name you may, only call it not an American rebellion; it is nothing more or less than a Scotch-Irish Presbyterian rebellion." So, needless to say, given their reported constitution, it took little time at all for the Ulster Presbyterians to become dissatisfied with their lot in County Down and turn their eyes to the western seas.

CHAPTER 2

Migration was a Family Affair

When the Scottish Presbyterians moved to Ireland, they were embarking on little more than a ferry crossing. They could see the Irish mainland from their home country, and the saltwater portion of the trip was barely 20 miles long. Boats came and left with regularity, and there would have been many firsthand reports of the lands they were about to inhabit—available housing, soil fertility, the prospects for success and such. It wasn't so much a voyage as a commute.

The colonies in America were different, requiring a leap of faith both figuratively and literally—literally, because the movement was driven largely by Presbyterian preachers who, along with their ministerial hats, wore the mantels of explorer, pioneer and warrior with equal aplomb. Ministers would preach resettlement from the pulpit, and entire congregations would pick up and move as one. Families would also sail across the Atlantic, either as a unit, or piecemeal. The McCulloghs were a part of this movement, as a study of the family history demonstrates; numerous members crossed the Atlantic and came to the Pennsylvania frontier.

Archibald McCullogh, five years older than James, was born in 1715, and seems to have been the pioneer immigrant of this branch

James McCullogh's Family Tree

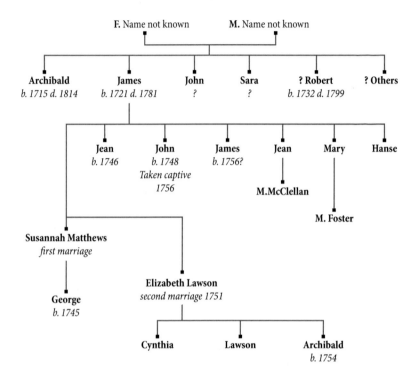

of McCulloghs, traveling from County Derry to Newcastle in what is now Delaware in about 1740. According to some genealogies, James had two other brothers, John, and possibly Robert, as there was a Robert who lived near James' home in Antrim Township, Pa. The boys had at least one sister, Sara, and possibly another whose name has been lost.

In his diary, James mentions Archibald, John, Sara and Robert. Archibald first married Susannah Matthews at the first Presbyterian Church in Philadelphia on April 11, 1740, and the couple had a son, George, born in 1745. A second marriage to Elizabeth Lawson on May 13, 1751, took place at the Old Swede's Church in New Castle, Del. Three children from this union are known: Cynthia, Lawson and Archibald (Archie), born in 1754. This is the Archie who was later scalped—he suffered brain damage, but survived—by the Indians during an attack at Enoch Brown School in Franklin County in 1764. The father Archibald was remembered in James McCullogh's will of 1778, when he devised to brother Archibald "my white coat and Sachel." Archibald lived until 1814, which would have made him 98 or 99 when he died in Kentucky.

Archibald's first son, George, who was born in New Castle, married Mary Crosby, who was born in 1749 in New Castle, and died in 1789 in Little Cove, Warren Township, Franklin County, Pa. They had one son, John, born in 1771 in New Castle, and who died in 1851 in Warren Township, near to Peters Township in Franklin County.

James McCullogh's brother, John McCullogh, is mentioned in a transaction in James' diary in 1749, suggesting that he lived nearby in the Marsh Creek settlement: "John McCullogh to an hog from mr James 16 shillings and 8 pence." And on the same page, "John McCullogh 15 shillings and 11 pence to James Priers vendow. (widow?)" An entry in the diary in 1756 notes that "John was killed May ye 26 in yr 56." As brother John McCullogh is never mentioned afterwards in the diary, this could have been James' brother John, but the diary is not specific and no historic corroboration is found.

James notes in his diary that he sold linen to his sister Sara in 1748, probably while living in the Marsh Creek area near Little's Run. One 1748 entry states,

"Sara McCullogh 40 yeards of bagin and 9 yeards if linsey 7 yeards stript and 3 yeards of shirting mor 40 yeards linen," and another entry relates "14 pence to John McCullogh upon Saras account and 13 yeards of shirting—15 pence and 69 pounds of Bef at two pence half peny per pound."

This could be the brother John, or Sara might have had a husband John). Then in June 1751, "Sara McCullough to 7 yeards of shirting woven and 9 yeards of lincey—5 yeards striped." In November 1751: "Sara McCullogh to 7s and on peny to tomas Montgomery." And, "December ye 6 1752 Sara McCullogh to 12 yeards of lincey—5 yeards striped with 3 shitels L 0-6-3." This shows the sister Sara was a regular customer for linen fabrics, at least while James was living in the Marsh Creek region south of Gettysburg, but not after James moves to Upton on the Conococheague.

Robert McCullogh, located in Antrim Township of Franklin County, is possibly the other brother. He was born about 1732, and appears on the Antrim Township tax records of 1753. He was buried in Greencastle after his death in 1779.

Other McCullogh names of unknown relationship show up in the Conococheague area, such as a William McCullogh on the Guilford Township (Chambersburg) tax records in 1753, and Samuel McCullogh, listed as an early settler in Antrim Township (Greencastle) in 1734.

Overall, where family was concerned, the entries in the diary demonstrate the close relationship that James had with his brothers and sister. Their dates of migration might have occurred in different years, but they all seem to have located in this same region on the Pennsylvania frontier. This was typical of the Scots-Irish, as the whole family tree was subject to move as a group. These families would have been inspired to a fever pitch by ministers at the pulpit, and later "runners" who would go into the Irish countryside to spread the word of the New World. James McCullogh does not disclose the reason for his decision to leave Ulster for America. But we know that his brother Archibald had already left by 1740.

There was much to do in anticipation of the move. Because of demand, passages were booked months in advance and, as the sailing date drew near, trunks would be packed and property, animals and machines were sold off. By the 1730s, transatlantic crossings were common—somewhere in the neighborhood of 1,500 a year—if not routine. But the western crossing was still six to eight weeks of torment. The stench alone would have been enough to put off most modern travelers, as seasickness, filth and rot built up over the long weeks in the overcrowded holds below decks. The meat was generally so sodden with salt that it was hard to recognize. Biscuits would break the teeth and the butter, after a couple of weeks, was usually rancid. There was little point in changing clothes or bathing, cooking was frequently out of the question on the rolling seas and the water was so contaminated that even the children drank beer—and they frequently died, anyway.

The men and women who populated Ulster certainly would have heard the stories and known what they were getting into. But they also knew they had a chance to own land instead of renting, where they were at the mercy of the landlord. They knew they could get out from under penal laws that discriminated against their religion. From all reports, the soil was fertile and a guarantee against hunger. The markets worked in favor of the small farmers and artisans, not against them. They knew there was a chance not just to exist but to get ahead. And they would have had reason to assume that there would be peace.

Moving to the New World took on a sense of urgency; there was a fear that they might be too late. The Scots-Irish had initially sailed for New England, but by 1719 word was coming back to Ulster that there was no longer any cheap land available for settlement. Maryland was rife with Catholics and New York and Virginia were not tolerant of dissenters. So the Ulster Presbyterians turned their attention to southern Pennsylvania, specifically a small settlement where a pacifist Quaker and champion of religious freedom named William Penn had first set foot on American soil in 1682.

CHAPTER 3

An Ocean Crossing and a New Life

After a decade of Oliver Cromwell and the Puritans, England in 1660 was ready for some levity. So they restored the "Merry Monarch," Charles II, son of the executed Charles I, to the throne. And just so there would be no confusion over where things stood, the monarchists dug up Cromwell's corpse (he had died of sepsis in 1658) and beheaded it on 30 January, 30, 1661, the 12th anniversary of the execution of Charles I.

Twenty years later, Charles II settled a financial debt he owed to the late William Penn, the naval officer, by ceding his son, also William, an eye-blinking amount of land, approximately 30 million acres, in the New World. Penn, a converted Quaker, was a tireless agitator for religious rights, so part of Charles' generosity might have been explained by a desire to get Penn out of England's hair. Whatever the case, both sides came out a winner.

Penn wasted no time in sailing off to see his new property, going ashore in New Castle, where the Delaware River flows into the Delaware Bay. Penn set up a colonial government and sailed 35 miles upriver to found the city of Philadelphia. As can be imagined, the Quaker government was not universally popular among more mainstream colonists in the lower part of the state, who eventually broke away in 1703 to found the state of Delaware, making New Castle the capital.

Penn died on the cusp of the great Scots-Irish immigration, but his legacy of religious tolerance and peace with the Native Americans persevered, at least for the time being. Pennsylvania became a melting pot of minority religions, some of which, including Amish and Mennonites, thrive to this very day. For the newly arriving Scots-Irish, Pennsylvania was indeed a promised land.

James McCullogh had purchased his logbook in Belfast and made note of his upcoming transoceanic adventure with his wife Martha, but then failed to follow up with any notation of his voyage. One final entry, apparently before he and his wife sailed read, "I went son a little whet December the 23 1745." The reader may make his or her own judgment about the meaning.

It appears that McCullogh sailed in the winter of 1746, most likely a year after he reserved passage. This would probably reflect the lengthy waiting list to get out of Ireland, whose leaders were watching with increasing agitation as the backbone of their economy was leaving en masse. In the mid-1730s, the British parliament considered legislation to block immigration as their tenants vacated their farms. Wealthy landlords threatened arrest and bodily harm against sea captains who sailed away with the landowners' meal tickets. The Irish courts, however, prudently refrained from interfering in commercial trade and travel.

By the time that James McCullogh left Ireland, his family had come through several years of famine brought on by an extremely cold year in 1740, followed by poor crops from even more cold rainy years. This famine was attended by typhus and dysentery epidemics that killed thousands of inhabitants. Despite this, it's worth noting that Ireland to the south in Dublin was prestigious enough that Handel first presented the "Messiah" there in 1745.

James and his wife were not in the class of indentured servants as they had paid for their passage in advance, and so established their place among the aristocracy of pioneer days. But the trip would still have been an arduous battle against storms and illness. it might be surprising to some of us that throughout the rest of the diary Martha is not mentioned in any way. It discloses a policy of not talking much about the female members of the family in colonial times. Col. Byrd of Virginia gives his opinion, rather harshly (but colorfully) about this attitude in his diary:

The men for their part, just like Indians, impose all the work upon the poor women. They make their wives rise out of their Beds early in the Morning, at the same time that they lye and Snore, till the sun has run one third of its course, and dispersed all the unwholesome Damps. Then after Stretching and Yawning for half an Hour, they light their Pipes, and under the Protection of a cloud of Smoak, venture out into the open Air; tho' if it ever happenst to be never so little cold, they quickly return Shivering into the chimney corner.

It is hard to believe that McCullogh went to this extreme.

On arriving in New Castle, he and his wife had the challenge of adjusting to a new country and finding a place to settle, aided, no doubt, by the Ulster Presbyterians or perhaps relatives who had come before and offered lodging and advice for their arriving brethren. There is no mention of farming in 1746 in New Castle, meaning the family had little time there to put down roots. The birth of his daughter Jean in New Castle in 1747 also went unremarked upon. But as McCullogh built a life on his new continent, his journal entries became more frequent.

He disembarked at New Castle, most likely, as many immigrants did, to avoid the loyalty oath that would have been required if he had disembarked at Philadelphia. New Castle itself at the time wasn't much—a single street lined with some brick buildings that included a couple of taverns, a court house, an Anglican church and, tucked into an ally, a Presbyterian meeting house that would have also served as a bank, hostel and travel-information center. But the condition of the town was irrelevant. The atmosphere would have been electric as passengers disembarked and turned their gaze to the west where the Blue Ridge Mountains awaited their arrival. From New Castle, McCullogh's young family gravitated 100 miles to the west, until their path was blocked by the nearly 2,000-foot South Mountain range, along a route that would become well worn by settlers seeking cheap land—when they paid for it at all. James Logan, a past secretary to Penn and future Philadelphia mayor, watched dumbfounded as ship after immigrant-packed ship sailed up the Delaware Bay. Writing to Penn's son, he grumbled that the newcomers "sitt frequently down on any spott of vacant Land they can find without asking questions."

But to be fair, they usually didn't "sitt" for long. Most, like McCullogh, sooner or later pressed on to the west, following an Indian warpath that in time became the Great Philadelphia Wagon Road.

Local records show that McCullough and Josiah Simpson acquired a tract of land in 1747 in Mount Joy Township, now Adams County. This was on the road now leading from Carlisle, Pa., to Baltimore, Md., as Gettysburg had not yet been founded. Little's Run ran along the south border of the tract. This tract was in the Marsh Creek settle

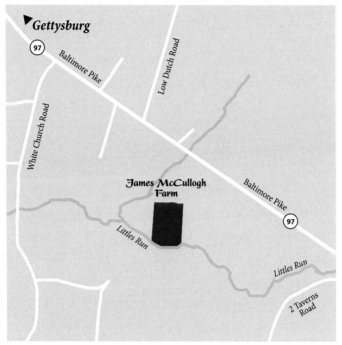

The location of James McCullogh's Adams County farm.

ment that was a part of the Manor of Maske, one of the largest manors in Pennsylvania in 1734. In this year the Penns authorized Lancaster County to issue two licenses on the two branches of Marsh Creek for settlement of unimproved lands west of the Susquehanna River, land that now lies in the central part of Adams County.

The Manor of Maske land was purchased from Iroquois Indians by 1737, which established a pattern that would come to haunt frontier settlers. The Iroquois had a habit of cutting deals among the colonies without including the resident Delaware Indians who would be affected. This sore spot would contribute to violence in years to come.

In the 1730s and 40s, the preponderance of settlers in Adams County were Scots-Irish. The Scots-Irish were also the main group of settlers in the Cumberland Valley, in what is now Cumberland County and Franklin County in south-central Pennsylvania. As such, the Scots-Irish were to play a role in what became an armed dispute between Maryland and Pennsylvania over the colonial line.

The curious affair had its roots in Pennsylvania's charter, which specified the boundary would extend north and west of New Castle on the 40th parallel. Unfortunately for the Penns, this put the southern part of Philadelphia squarely in Maryland, a situation that Maryland's Calvert family was more than happy to accept. The Penns, of course didn't see it that way—they claimed land south to below Annapolis, Md.—and proposed a boundary that fit the spirit of the law, if not the letter—and brought Philadelphia comfortably back into the fold.

The dispute became so contentious that in 1730 hostilities erupted among tough frontiersmen who really didn't need much of an excuse for a fight. In the so-called Cresap's War, named for Thomas Cresap, Lord Baltimore's land agent, militias of both colonies were called in, touching off a series of minor property spats. It took King George II's intervention to end the shooting part of the conflict. By the time McCullogh arrived, a tentative agreement basically split the difference between the contested boundary lines, but the issue really wasn't settled until Charles Mason and Jeremiah Dixon surveyed their famous line in the 1760s.

The upshot, however, was that the Ulster Presbyterians who had been looked down upon by the Quakers were now, if not newly loved, at least newly useful. Both Maryland and Pennsylvania sought to bolster their claims to the disputed territory by populating the lands with

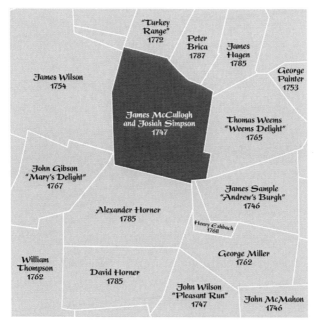

When James McCullogh bought the Mt. Joy farm with Josiah Simpson, the only bordering tract was that of "Andrews Burgh" owned by James Sample. Note the purchase dates of the other bordering properties.

colonists. McCullogh stayed on the Scots-Irish Pennsylvania side as Maryland had mostly German settlers south of the line.

The purchase of his Mt. Joy farmland so soon after his arrival suggests that James had come to America with cash in hand. The only bordering tract that pre-dates this purchase was a tract owned by James Sample called "Andrews Burgh," dating to 1746. Later neighbors were a Wilson in 1754, and one Thomas Weems in 1765.

In August 1747—the year he bought his land at auction—there is a diary entry, "I did reap ray" (i.e. rye). Was this already a crop on his new farm? Or had he arrived on this farm earlier and taken a period of time to complete the purchase? In 1749, the diary says he sowed rye, wheat and buckwheat, which we conclude was on this farm at Marsh Creek.

On May 27, 1748, McCullogh wrote, "son John born, it being Friday about one o'clock on the 12th day of the moon's age." He carried on farming and engaged in the linen trade at Marsh Creek through 1752. Of the 20 or more people recorded in his diary, only a couple can be located on tract maps or tax records of the adjoining townships. Many were probably squatters or he may have been selling to people farther away than his immediate neighbors.

His crops in 1750 were turnips sown on July 4 and again on July 23. Oats were reaped on July 5. On July 10, he began plowing for wheat and began to sow wheat on August 29, completing the task on September 13. This sowing day seems to be an unusually early date when compared to present-day practices. However, the weather may have been cooler then as this was toward the end of the Little Ice Age, and they were still using the old Julian calendar at this time. When Great Britain and the colonies adopted the Gregorian calendar in September 1752, the switch resulted in a loss of 11 days. An entry on October 20 noted that all corn and fodder was in, an activity that was presumably timed on the Julian calendar. This may explain the seemingly early date here.

In 1751, flax was planted on March 20 and threshed on July 19 for seed. Corn was planted from April 23 to April 29. A week after the birth of his second son, James Jr., McCullogh records that 32 shocks of rye were harvested on June 19, and 126 shocks of wheat on June 26. These numbers suggest that McCullogh's crops had increased considerably over several years as he became an established agricultural success. Yet an American tenet was to always think bigger and better; James McCullogh had done well on his first farm—who knew how much further he could take his business on his second, one that would be located in the fertile valley along a steep gully that flowed into the Conococheague?

CHAPTER 4

The Frontier Beckons

James McCullogh does not specifically say why he picked up and moved farther west to the Allegheny frontier, although the decision almost certainly would have had something to do with land, and possibly with religion. In 1752 at a sheriff's sale, James McCullogh bought a farm near the west branch of the Conococheague Creek, about two miles south of present-day Upton. This new farm was about 40 miles from his Marsh Creek farm. It appears the year 1753 was spent in transition to this new farm, as his crops were meager for that year. The new farm, located on the present Weaver Road, had a gully passing through a portion of it, but some hillside land was available for flax and other crops. It sat upon a wooded ridge that ran north and south parallel to the Kittochitinny Mountain range.

Coming to Conocheague six years after he landed at New Castle, McCullogh seems to have been accompanied by other family members, at least two brothers and a sister who are known to have helped with his farming and linen operations. In addition to raising the regular subsistence-grain crops and pasture, he specialized in raising flax for spinning linen, skills he had learned before leaving Northern Ireland.

James McCullogh continued to farm at this site for years, developing a sizable linen business.

His closest neighbors are not known, because many immigrants in those days were squatters and delayed or avoided altogether going through the process to take out a patent or title to their land. There was no town or village nearby, as Upton and Welsh Run were not yet village settlements and Greencastle would not be founded for more than 20 years. There were no shops or stores, just distant trading posts and itinerant traders. James McCullogh brought along molasses and other articles purchased from Thomas Montgomery in Adams County. In "The Colonial Military Organization of Lower Path Valley" in the Kittochtinny Historical Society Papers, edited by Fred Shearer, it seems that a Jacob Pyatte had a mountain trading post in Path Valley between Dry Run and Concord before 1738.

Three to four miles to the west of James McCullogh lived what might have counted as a neighbor, a physician, Hugh Mercer, who had trained in Scotland and emigrated to America following the Battle of Cullodon, the final confrontation of the 1745 Jacobite Rising. The frontier at this place and time had a smattering of people, but in the main lacked strength in numbers.

The immigrants used trails that had been established by the Native Indians. The Great Valley Trail served as a major route south from Harris's Ferry (Harrisburg) through the Cumberland Valley, somewhat following high ground near the East branch of the Conococheague Creek, continuing south to the Potomac at Wadkins Ferry, now Williamsport, Md. A branch trail took off westward at Pawling's Tavern, fording the main branch of the Conococheague Creek near the future

Mason-Dixon Line. It followed the west side of the west branch past the meetinghouse of the Lower West Presbyterian Church near Welsh Run. This church was two or three miles west of the farm of James McCullogh.

The Indian trail continued northwest to Black's Town, now Mercersburg, and north along the west branch of the Conococheague, eventually into Indian country to Path Valley and on to the Allegheny Mountains. Mercersburg would not be laid out for another 20 years, but wagon roads were gradually evolving. The first major road, Forbes Road, ran southward from Carlisle in the north past Parnell Knob to Fort Loudon, and was cut beginning in 1755. But even this crude road, described as not very satisfactory because it was stony and brushy, was more than five miles away from McCullogh's farm.

James McCullogh does not mention the route he followed from Marsh Creek to Upton, but whatever route he took would have been rudimentary, too, hardly more than a horse path, unable to accommodate wagons. One established route he might have taken would have led through Fairfield, Pa., across the Blue Ridge Mountains at Blue Ridge Summit through the steep, tricky Monterey Pass, and from there to Upton. About 19 years later, this trail became an offshoot of the Philadelphia Wagon Road, which merged with the Great Valley Trail north of Williamsport, Md. But in the middle of the eighteenth century, it is quite probable that the McCulloghs would have set out across the mountains not with a wagon, but with pack animals, which severely limited the capacity for baggage and equipment. Reports of women clamoring along rugged mountain trails carrying their spinning wheels are not unheard of. Farther south, this trail crossed the

Potomac into the Shenandoah Valley, a route that was used by thousands of migrant settlers to the south, including celebrated pioneers such as Daniel Boone.

The Scots-Irish neighbors in the Cumberland Valley had largely come by a northern route through Donegal, crossing the Susquehanna River at Harris' Ferry and continued on south. The Scots-Irish established a series of meetinghouses in the Cumberland Valley, reaching this area by 1737 at the Falling Springs Church (Chambersburg), Moss Springs (Greencastle) and the West Conococheague Meeting (Church Hill) in 1738. A New Light congregation seceded from the Church Hill group to form the Lower West Conococheague meeting in 1741 (the New Light movement was an evangelical movement that swept the countryside as part of the first Great Awakening in British North America).

McCullogh's farm was situated between these two churches on the west branch of the Conococheague Creek. The Scots-Irish settlers to the north and west of McCullogh's farm were the McDowell, Maxwell, McClure, McClellan and Irwin families. To the south were some Welsh settlers extending as far south as the Potomac (the Shelbys) and southwest to the Appalachian valleys and coves (closed valleys surrounded by high mountains), including David Davis and Rees Shelby. Welsh settlers also included John Davis, a Seventh-Day Baptist, and Philip Davis of Fort Philip Davis, a Presbyterian, who were close by in Welsh Run. Other Welsh settlers included the Blairs of Blair Valley, Bowens, Rosses, David Evans and a number of other families. Very few German families were nearby at this early date, with no record of Mennonites or Amish. This is the context of the region when James McCullogh came.

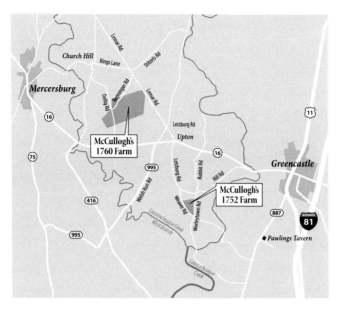

The locations of the McCullogh farms in the area of the West branch of the Conococheague. The early farm was 1752-1760, the later farm 1760-1786.

The land here was fertile, and the immigrants must have known that it was superior to the land in the other areas. There were open grasslands in the Cumberland Valley that would have been easier to farm. The large trees in the forest were also a valuable resource, including large oak, walnut and chestnuts, with an understory of spice bushes and rich forbs on the ground. There were many limestone outcroppings with plenty of springs nearby, both indicators of good farmland. Native Americans who had lived in the Welsh Run region might have been unwitting allies of the new farmers, having in past decades burned over some of the forest area, creating open barrens. Indians set fires for a variety of reasons, from reinvigorating berry bushes to providing browse for wildlife to enhancing hunting, and even for pest control.

While Seneca Indians came from the New York area to the fork of the Conococheague for hunting and in late winter for maple syrup, but there is no record of established Indian villages.

Still, the work necessary to carve out a farm would have been backbreaking. Most likely, McCullogh, like other Scots-Irish settlers, would have traveled in a group of family members and/or fellow Ulster Presbyterians who would share the work involved in making a new start. His diary entries show he had regular helpers.

The mountains to the west of McCullogh's farm were considered an obstacle to the immigrants, who did not try to cross them but settled on the eastern borders and coves. Indian paths crisscrossed the mountains and followed the valleys, trails that the European Indian traders explored and gladly used. The immigrants who ventured into these areas were Welsh, who established the Seventh Day Baptists churches in Little Cove, Tonolway and the Great Cove.

Without roads, the immigrants crossing the valley followed mountain landmarks. Two peaks of the Kittochtinny Range were readily visible from the McCullogh farm, landmarks that were visible all across the Cumberland Valley as far as the Blue Ridge range 30 to 40 miles away. The one to the northwest was Parnell's Knob, which stood at the southern end of the range on the east side of the west branch of the Conococheague Creek in Path Valley. An Indian trail followed this branch of the Conocoheague Creek 20 miles north before crossing west near present Fort Littleton. Another landmark, Kaisie's Knob, was visible to the southwest. The flatland between was called "The Cove."

In the Little Cove, the Welshman David Davis built a private fort in 1756 for protection. Between these landmarks and James Mc-

Cullogh's farm, a number of settlers had found the limestone soil very good for farming. There were several parallel forested ridges to the west of James McCullogh's, where the trees were tall and provided excellent timber for buildings. During the summer the forests were filled with passenger pigeons with many large trees supporting numerous nests. The now-extinct doves filled the air with their calls in the summer and in the fall, the story goes, formed flocks so large that they blocked out the sun.

Once the land had been chosen, cabins were thrown together, trees cut, stumps pulled and some semblance of crops would be planted. The manual labor involved would have been almost incomprehensible by today's standards; for example, zigzag fencing in a single acre of land would have required splitting 800 rails.

But while the land required hard work, it also had plenty to give back. Wildlife was abundant, with those dense summer populations of passenger pigeons, the streams full of fish and shellfish, and a variety of such animals as deer, beaver, mink, elk and even Eastern Woodland bison. As a result, as the good land was taken, the newcomers had to move southward down the Great Valley Trail across the Potomac River at Wadkins Ferry (Williamsport) in their search for land in western Virginia, North Carolina, South Carolina, and Georgia, or through the Cumberland Gap to Kentucky and Tennessee.

Not mentioned in the diary, but perhaps a motivating factor for James McCullogh in choosing this location was a minister, the Rev. John Steel of the Upper West Conococheague Presbyterian Church. This was a practicing Old Side Presbyterian church, the established church that stuck to strict Calvinistic principles. Rev. Steel was born in Newton, Londonderry, Ireland in 1715. He came from Scotland as a probationer, that is, a not-yet-ordained preacher, and his name shows up in 1736 in the minutes of the Presbytery of Donegal. In 1744, he was ordained by the Presbytery at New Castle, where he served from 1744 to 1752 (recall that McCullogh arrived in New Castle in 1746 and must have heard Steel's church services). In 1752, Steel moved to the Conococheague area, where he was in charge of two congregations, the one at Church Hill (long known as the Presbyterian White Church) and one in Greencastle. James McCullogh chose to be a member at Church Hill rather than the closer meetinghouse at Welsh Run. Steel joined the Pennsylvania militia and served from 1756 to 1758. For Steel, it was not enough just to fight for the Lord. He fought Indians, trafficked in weapons and later agitated for the American Revolution.

After the family moved to Upton, the next McCullogh child to be born was Elizabeth in 1753, and then Mary in 1755—so both of these were born before the French and Indian War disturbances occurred. The last known child was Hance, born around 1757. Daughter Jean married a man named McClellan and had a son, James McClellan. One of the other daughters married a man named Harren, and had two children, Jannet and Rachel Harren—that information is gleaned from James McCullogh's will.

In June 1752, James notes that Jean "did enter to skool Jun ye 15, 1752 & did only 6 days at that time." Later in 1758, he writes "Jean McColoch did enter John Robisons scol upon Tuesday ye 17th of July and was 4 days ye first week at scull." This seems to have been in the Upton region.

McCullogh's house was described as standing on a bluff on the east side of a point where three ravines converge. In March 1753 he built a "berreck," probably a hay barrack, a structure that generally included four tall posts with a roof that could be moved up and down as the quantity of hay in need of protection dictated. In June 1753, he built a sheep house. By 1754 he was back to producing a sizable linen crop and his entries show a settler who was establishing a considerable commercial enterprise:

— In May 1754 he sold to "Ephraim Smith … 19 yeards of linen October ye 22 and 9 yeards of blanket ye 23 day of October."

— "Ephraim Smith to 3 yeards of linen woven March ye 30th 1755 to 10 yeards of wollen October ye 21 (probably 1754)."

— "May 1754 Adam Armstrong to weaving of shirtin 15 shillings to 8 yeards bagin."

— "July 8th of 2 days reaping July 17 to one day of reaping wheat to 35 yeards lincey woven in February 1756".

— "Colen Spence 60 yeards of linen woven in March 1755 & 17 yeards of bagin in Apriel & 10 yeards of covering &1 bushel of flax seed & 2 yeards of girthing and 25 yeards of linen jun 19 yeards of hikrey in may 18 yeards of lincey".

— "Thomas Deveson to 58 yeards of linen woven May ye 14 1755."

These entries are telling, because they show McCullogh to be a businessman, not just a subsistence farmer. He had brought his skills as a weaver from the old country, and was rapidly establishing himself as an important player in the commerce of south-central Pennsylvania.

But crops and weaving weren't the only thing on the McCulloghs' minds. There were rumors that Indians, agitated that the pioneers were farming on their land, were coming to settle an old score. McCullogh wrote in his diary, "July ye 12 1755 was put to flight by a fals alarm from ye ingens." While the Indians didn't show on this particular occasion, it wouldn't be long before they did.

CHAPTER 5

Pioneer Agriculture

Prior to the first eruption of Indian violence in 1755, James Mc-Cullogh was able to develop a good agricultural track record; rare information is found in McCullogh's logs concerning his crops, revealing the agricultural practices on the colonial Pennsylvania frontier. An early entry on his first arrival—"bushel of ray And 1 bushel of pota-tous and one half bushel of corn November 1746"—perhaps suggests that he had arrived in America early enough in the year to have these crops. The location of his farm is not stated, but it was presumably somewhere near New Castle. He did some scant farming in 1746, as in November of that year he planted one bushel of rye. He would have barely had time to harvest in in the ensuing summer, because it appears that he bought land and presumably moved to Lancaster County in 1747.

In July 1748, "we did sow turnips July 22 yet ... Sara 14 and 4 yeards." An interpretation might be that he had limited space or tillable soil, as there is no mention of other crops. And was his sister, Sara, nearby? In 1749 he planted rye (he spells it "ray" representing the Scottish pronunciation) on June 18, wheat on June 23 and buckwheat on July 3. In 1750 he sowed flax on March 23 and oats April 3. Wheat was harvested July 3, with a sickle and cradle. Flax and buckwheat were sown on June 28. More buckwheat was sown on July 11, and he "thrush flax July the 12th." An entry dated Sept. 13, 1750, records that turnips were sown July 4 and oats reaped July 5; turnips were sown July 23, he began plowing August 10, and began to sow wheat August 29, completing it by September 13. (For wheat, the soil was plowed and the seeds scattered by hand). This sowing date for wheat was quite a bit earlier than present-day practices. A later entry notes that all the corn and fodder was in by October 20. The amount of land in crops seems to show a big increase from 1749 to 1750.

In 1751, his farming pattern was similar to 1750, planting flax on March 20, with threshing of flax on July 19. He planted corn from April 23 to April 29. Rye was harvested June 17 and wheat June 26, yielding 126 shocks of wheat and 23 shocks of rye. On July 8 he reaped oats and on July 11 he cut hay. These crop dates are not much different today.

Having cleared marshland in December 1750, "I did sow my New meadow Agust ye 16 and 17th 1751." Combining flax with other crops was a practice McCullogh would have brought from Ireland, where the price on linen fluctuated severely and at times dropped below the cost of production. Weavers diversified their crops to protect against the bad times; in good times, these staples put food on the table and more or less subsidized the linen operation, allowing the Scots-Irish to undersell their competitors.

In 1752 he goes into more detail on how long it took to put in a crop using the plows of that time. "I did plow nine days and a half myself in corn. On May 7, "I did sow nine bushels and a half of oats and planted 12 bushels of corn I did finist (finish) planting corn on May ye 7 and planted potatous said day 13 days of plowing and harrowing befor planting & 3 spels (spells) plowing in ye upper field 2 plowing and 4 spels in ye far field and 3 spels in ye field over the meadow." And then, "We had done moulding corn June ye 11th 1752 (shallow plowing for weeds uses the plow's moulding plate after the coulter plate, the blade used for deep cutting into the soil, has been removed).

To summarize, during these years of farming in the Marsh Creek settlement, the crops mentioned were wheat, rye, corn, oats, buckwheat and turnips. For his flax crops he tried various planting dates. In 1748 he planted on June 27; in 1750 he sowed August 25 to September 11; in 1751 he planted August 20 to September 11, and then in 1752 he planted flax on March 31 in the spring, which was the schedule he used from then on. The harvesting time in in the summer, in July, allowed time for the drying and retting in hot weather.

In 1753 there was a gap in the entries on farming, presumably the year when he moved to the Conococheague farm. There was the process of moving equipment and livestock over poor roads from Marsh Creek to the Upton farm. It is not known whether he did some farming and did not have the time to keep his diary, or was not able to get the land ready in time for that year's crops. In July 1754, he resumes making some entries. An entry of July 16 reads, "I did reap ray at Sam torentines and cut my leg said day July 6 1954 to one day & half reaping July ye 15 and 16th days."

Finding markets for his crops would have been another issue. The Upton farm stood in a frontier area that was only recently and lightly settled by the 1750s. The only commercial establishment in the region was Pawling's Tavern, which was a junction for packhorse trains. In this context there were no stores of any type—no mills, and no practical way to send crops or produce to market. The McCulloghs were engaged in subsistence farming, where a household had to produce or make all their own food, clothing and equipment.

Roads consistent with commerce were slow in developing. By 1761, the Great Valley Trail had a wagon road of sorts, which was passable in good weather. Probably the first road going west through this part of Franklin County was a branch of the Broadfording Road. After fording the Conococheague Creek, the route turned north crossing into Pennsylvania at Fairview, Md., and then followed Locust Level Road onto a new road laid out around 1765 to 1768 through Welsh Run, that went west to Mercersburg. This region of the west branch of the Conococheague Creek had more farms and settlers than much of the land in the central part of the Cumberland Valley, where the soil was not as good. And the Scots-Irish who had migrated down the Cumberland Valley established church meetinghouses every 11 miles, give or take. In all, it apparently was enough of a population to support McCullogh's linen business.

The diary does not disclose how good the crops were in the year 1754. But he is planning ahead and "had done seeding wheat October ye 22 1754." In 1755 the notes are again scant. Of interest is a note of May, noting, "94b29t 7cCays whit hefer did take bul Maye 28th 1755." James had a number code for some of the alphabet that he used from time to time, probably for secrecy. This refers to Robert McCay's white heifer, which he mated with the bull. His notes show that he began to plant corn June 23, which is late for planting that particular crop. He finished reaping rye on July 19, and he finished reaping wheat July 12 with "803 dozen in ye new land, and did get all in July ye 19. An ominous note follows, dated Aug. 14, 1755, stating, "a fort at ye meeting hous was begun July ye 30." The British had just been routed by the French and Indians on the Monongahela River near present-day Pittsburgh, and the pioneers suspected the worst. They were right. The following two years, 1756 and 1757, were most disruptive for Mc-Cullogh's farming and linen business, and it was not until 1758 that he resumed documenting his farm operation.

CHAPTER 6

Terror on the Frontier

For many years there had been peaceful coexistence in the Mid Atlantic colonies among the Native Americans and the Europeans who were settling on the Indian homelands. When William Penn arrived in 1682, he met with the native Lenape (Delaware) tribe in order to establish friendship and a fair working relationship. When he negotiated a price for settlement tracts in this colony of Pennsylvania, the Eastern Lenape were able to move to other lands further west. However, William Penn's descendants were not so considerate, negotiating with the Iroquois for lands that the Lenape were using as homelands. As the Iroquois, British and French bartered over these homelands, the Delaware were left out in the cold.

One particular act, the Walking Purchase in 1737 (so-named because the land in question was the distance that one man could walk in a day and a half), particularly angered the Lenape, as it was viewed—probably with justification—as cheating them of their homeland. The Lenape had to move quite a distance to the west and established a new tribal area with its central town or capital at Kittanning, along the Allegheny River. But their tribe had been weakened and disorganized and the territory was not good farm country, so it was difficult for them to prosper. And to make matters worse, some Scots-Irish settlers ignored any negotiated boundary lines and moved into areas that quite clearly still belonged to the Indians. As a result, they had many grievances, and when the opportunity presented they were eager to seek revenge.

Multiple circumstances culminating in 1755 allowed them this chance. First, the Pennsylvania colony was Quaker-governed and the Pennsylvania Assembly was dominated by pacifists who were not amenable to establishing any official military forces to protect the colony. Seeing the need, Benjamin Franklin had established a voluntary militia in 1749 in Philadelphia. But there were no organized forces on the frontier, only local brigades that were poorly provided for (many had no shoes), and poorly armed.

There were other slights as well that fed the anger of the Lenape (Delawares). With the Iroquois dominating Pennsylvania territories, the Delawares could not find a satisfactory way to make their concerns heard. In the meantime, the Native Americans' issues were relegated to the back burner by the conflict that was building between the English and the French over the territory west of the Appalachian Mountains.

The French were attempting to establish dominion over the territory between their trading posts on the St. Lawrence River in Canada and those on the Mississippi north of New Orleans. The British wanted this territory for access to Native American trading posts and land for settlements. Virginia went so far as to claim title to the portion of Pennsylvania west of the Appalachians and. on May 28, 1754, a 22-year-old militia officer by the name of George Washington picked an unfortunate fight with the French in a remote corner of the state. Sent by Virginia Gov. Robert Dinwiddle to protect the colony's interests, Washington's men ambushed a handful of French and Indian scouts, and a heartbreaking series of misunderstandings—precipitated by the language barrier between the English and French speakers—touched off the Seven Years War, a global conflict that is better known here as the French and Indian War.

Into this pressure cooker stepped Gen. Edward Braddock, who sailed into the mouth of the Chesapeake Bay in Virginia on Feb. 20, 1755, with two regiments of Scot Highlanders in the British forces. With their arrival, the settlers were hopeful that the frontier would be protected both from the French and from the Indians. As things turned out, it had the opposite effect.

Two months later in Alexandria, Braddock and colonial governors agreed on several simultaneous military expeditions against the French, including the general's own campaign to take Fort Duquesne near present-day Pittsburgh. Funding the campaign was a problem from the beginning and so was the terrain. Heading west from Frederick, Md. to the Virginia territory, Braddock's regulars were pressed into the position of highway engineers and lumberjacks, cutting a trail through the mountain wilderness.

It is fascinating to note that the history of great nations was being written by a few hundred men slugging it out in a vast wilderness that was several days' travel from anything resembling civilization.

Ironically, Braddock's force greatly outnumbered the French and Indian allies who rushed out from the banks of the Monongahela River on July 9 to block the British advance, but his men were not prepared for the wilderness engagement. They were sandwiched in on a primitive road, which allowed the French and Indians picked them off from the cover of the forest. Washington accompanied Braddock on the expedition and ably rallied the troops after Braddock was shot. Washington put Braddock's strength at 1,300 men, and the enemy at a mere 300. Despite the favorable odds the fight was a full-blown rout, with more than 900 British soldiers killed or wounded. Back in England, author Horace Walpole tartly noted that the battle set the record for being the longest continuous fight against nobody. Braddock died of his wounds four days later. He went to his grave baffled at how such a scant, ragtag opponent could have dealt trained British soldiers such a humiliating blow, and his dying words to Washington were said to be a bewildered "Who would have thought?"

Flush with victory, the French lost no time in goading the Indians into attacking frontier settlers. It was an easy sell since the Indians wished to force the European settlers off the lands that were still considered Indian territory. This included all land west of the 1736 demarcation line on the eastern slope of the Allegheny ranges. A scant three days after Braddock's defeat, rumors of Indian attacks were flying. Settlers responded to the threat of impending Indian attack by fortifying homes and churches. On July 30, McCullogh noted that "a fort at ye meetinghouse was begun July ye 30." This refers to the Presbyterian meetinghouse that McCullogh attended at Church Hill where Rev. Steel was minister and oversaw the fortifying of the palisade surrounding the church.

Back in the Monongahela wilderness, the British troops who were able made a disorganized and demoralized retreat from the region under the command of Col. Thomas Dunbar. Dunbar, still in possession of a significant numerical advantage, had no taste for rejoining the battle; instead, he skedaddled back east, barely slowing until he reached Philadelphia, leaving behind junked wagons and equipment in a gully.

McCullogh records this history concerning the retreating troops: "Cornel Dunbar and his armey did camp at henry pollens agust 13 1755," noting that the troops who were retreating from the west had completed their trek through Fort Wills (Cumberland) and passed above Winchester. They then turned north across the Potomac and up the Great Valley Trail to Pawling's Tavern.

Pawling's Tavern was at the mouth of the Conococheague, where the army crossed the Potomac on their march north (see map on page 45). Pawling's stood on a grassy meadow beside a spring and a stream, about two miles south of present-day Greencastle. Pawling had settled and set up a campsite at an intersection of packhorse trails. His house stood near the Great Valley Trail, the route Dunbar was taking. Another trail to the west started here, winding west along the west branch of the Conococheague Creek to the region of Upton, and to Mercersburg to meet other trails over the mountains.

The crossroads that Dunbar slogged through was about five miles directly east of James McCullogh's farm. The settlers on the far outposts of the colonial frontier could have been excused for a sinking feeling in their stomachs as they watched their best hope of defense disappear over the horizon. The British troops had stirred up a hornet's nest and then ignominiously fled, leaving the frontier colonists to fend for themselves. It would be one more reason for the Scots-Irish to despise the monarchy and take up the banner of independence in another 20 years.

For a time, there is a paucity of entries in the McCullogh diary recorded that summer, as Braddock's defeat signaled a clear and present danger of Indian retaliation—and they did indeed become an ever-greater distraction in the latter part of 1755. But as the attacks became more personal and hit closer to home, McCullogh's chronicles of Indian encounters picked up noticeably, as did the attacks themselves. Considering all of the efforts that James McCullogh made to protect his family from dangers of the times, it is ironic that in the end he was unable to do so. Another irony is that Presbyterian ministers who had led McCullogh and his compatriots to the promised land were now called into duty as warriors, not for their Lord, but for the colonists.

The frontier minister Charles Beatty, for one, tirelessly promoted the virtues the New World (as well as his own virtues) to Ulster Scots back home, so his crestfallen reaction to the changing landscape is understandable:

> A savage & barbarous Enemy, prompted by the pernicious French, like prowling wolves fell on the Peaceful Habitations of many of our Frontier Inhabitants, and in the Night, time after time, murdered and scalped without regard to Age or Sex, and led numbers of our people into captivity, who are many of them on bondage among the Heathen to this Day. As the Frontier Counties of Pennsylvania and Virginia were mostly settled by people of our Denomination, we felt the Blow severely; several of our congregations were entirely broken up; the Ministers removed to other Provinces., or sought shelter in the innermost part of the Provinces distressed by the War, or went forth with their People to repel the enemy Among these our Worthy Agent, the Reverend Mr Charles Beatty distinguished himself by his public Spirit, Love to his Country and true Courage."

This was the sort of violence the Ulster Scots had left their homeland to get away from. An important feature of McCullogh's diary is the record kept of Indian attacks and atrocities on this part of the Appalachian frontier during the French & Indian War years. It is a story of being in the right place at the right time, as far as being an eyewitness to history is concerned. But the McCullogh family wouldn't have seen it this way; for them it was the opposite—being in the wrong place, in the midst of a war between the Native Americans, the displaced Delaware, and the settlers who occupied the Indian territory, their historic hunting grounds.

It was an ironic turn to James' vision of a new life full of freedom and success. But he persisted with his intent to live on the frontier and to weave cloth. During this time of disruption, many of those who had settled on this frontier fled, including the McCullogh family; some returned as the McCulloghs did, some didn't. As the hostilities escalated, many sought refuge to the east.

In November, the first catastrophe struck the Conococheague region, just over Tuscarora Mountain to the west in the Great Cove, a picturesque valley extending from the Maryland border north to the present-day town of McConnellsburg in Fulton County.

On Saturday, Nov. 1, 1755, contingent of 100 Shawnee and Delaware Indians led both by Frenchmen and Delaware King Shingas (dubbed "Shingas the Terrible" by settlers) began their attack near what is now Hancock, Md., sweeping north through Great Cove, burning many barns and houses, slaughtering livestock and killing any settler unlucky enough to be at home when the attackers arrived.

McCullogh, reported, "Ye great cove was burnt & our flight to Mash Creek was Novr ye 2 1755." He included a list summarizing the number of residents of the Big Cove killed and the number taken. He believed that 77 had been killed, and there was notation of "t-49," which might stand for taken or missing.

And even though Fort Ahl, in present Fulton County, had been constructed in Great Cove near McConnellsburg, the devastation was so great that the many survivors fled back east and had to be accommodated at Rev. Steel's Fort at Church Hill. The attack was brutal, and a nineteenth century history told of an elderly woman whose body was found impaled on a stake with one breast cut off. Eyewitnesses to the attack stated that following the attack Great Cove effectively ceased to exist as a colonial settlement.

It should be noted, however, that the inhabitants of the Great Cove were squatters on Indian land that was west of the established boundary of the 1736 purchase. In 1750, when Cumberland County was established, squatters were expelled from the Path Valley region by the new County Sheriff and cabins were burnt. But squatters remained to the south and west. In 1754, the Penns acquired the lands from the Delaware that extended ownership into the Allegheny Mountains, the last extension of the inhabitable borders of the colony. This attack, therefore, was essentially an effort by the Indians to remove illegal immigrants from their land, and push them back east. In the year 1755, the Indian attacks were in the regions west of the legal occupation. But in 1756, some of the attacks crossed this 1736 boundary back into the area where settlers may have thought they were safe.

As James and Martha now had five small children, he feared for their safety following the Great Cove attack and left the farm at Upton to go back to Marsh Creek, most likely to wait out an expected attack on the east side of the mountains in the Mercersburg area. Before he left his farm, he wrote that he hid his equipment, including a "pitch-fork, pulty (pulley), gers (gears), against sheephouse," and salt, plow-shears and cleves under the hay barrack.

McCullogh left for safer ground in November when crop farming was over. However, he needed to make arrangements for care of his livestock; farm helpers mentioned in his diary, who could well have been indentured servants, probably performed this work. His diary indicates that he returned to the area on Dec. 17.

The Indians seized the advantage in 1756, attacking settlers east of the Tuscarora and Kittatinny Mountains where colonists had been coming legally since the 1736 treaty. Many of the settlers had Blun-ston licenses, a sort of preliminary license, from the clerk of Lancaster County, giving them warrants to their farms and permission to have surveys to seek deeds.

In 1756, the diary begins by recording a raid in February: "John Creag Richert and John cocks (Cox) was taken by Indins feberwary 11."

But another Indian attack in nearby Welsh Run was not, curious-ly, mentioned in the diary; it occurred on March 2, when the Hein-rich Studebaker farm was attacked. Heinrich, who had a gun leaning against a tree, was clearing stumps off his farm when he was killed before he could reach his weapon. His older son, Joseph, who had been helping him pull stumps, was captured while running toward the house. The Indians then went to the farmhouse and seized his pregnant wife and infant child, his five-year-old daughter Elizabeth, and his 10-year-old son Philip. They were led up the Back Creek and then over the mountain range to Path Valley. The pregnant wife, now a widow, fell behind and was killed and scalped by the Indians. The children became aware of her fate when they noticed that one of the Indians bring up the rear was wearing her hat.

After arrival in Kittanning, the children were bathed in a creek to clean off the evil heritage and then adopted into Indian families in the Ohio region. Indian culture was a world apart from the European. And with the maternal hierarchy, the disciplinarian of the family would be the maternal uncle.

Philip Studebaker was among a small group released in 1762 during negotiations in Lancaster. He was met there by his older sister, Susannah, who was not taken captive, and by their uncle, Allen Killough. The other Studebaker daughter, Elizabeth, and older brother, Joseph Studebaker, were among the 82 prisoners returned at Lower Shawnee Town at the mouth of the Scioto River in November 1764. Joseph was returned to the Conococheague, but sister, Elizabeth, refused. She went back to live with their Indian families.

It is curious that James McCullogh's diary did not include a reference to this attack, which occurred only a few miles away on the south side of the Conococheague Creek. Is this an omission due to fear and pain over a tragedy so nearby? From the diary one can conclude that the McCulloghs were in Upton at the time, because a month later he mentions fleeing the area again. "We did move all to Anttetem April ye 19 1756." This refers to the Antietam settlement, near present Waynesboro, Pa., which is on the east side of the Cumberland Valley and not as arduous a trek from Upton as climbing over the Blue Ridge Mountains to Marsh Creek near Gettysburg. Research has uncovered an Alexander McCullogh living at Marsh, a settlement in Maryland territory along the Antietam Creek, which begins some miles north in Pennsylvania with two branches, the East Branch and the West Branch, which join south of present-day Waynesboro.

The forts in general proximity to James McCullogh's farm.

As the year progressed, Indian attacks and kidnappings increased. On April 1 there was a Delaware attack on Fort McCord northeast of Parnell Knob. Among the families seeking refuge and safety, there was John Lowery, his wife and five children. John was killed and the family was marched west over the ranges to Path Valley. John's scalp conspicuously swung from the hand of a warrior. A rescue party caught up with the departing Indians, and the battle of Sideling Hill ensued, only to see the death of would-be rescuers.

The mother, Jean McCord Lowery, wrote *A Journal of the Captivity of Jean Lowry and her Children* (published by the Conococheague Institute), describing her experiences as captive after her return to freedom in 1760. She also provides "horrific details of Indian scalping,

69

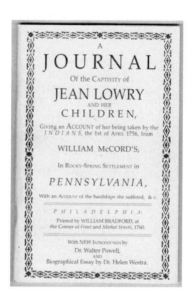

burning, and killing of prisoners at Sidling Hill, as well as graphic accounts of the captives' physical torments and sufferings as they travel."
Her three older children, ages 6, 8, and 10 were separated from her one
by one to be adopted by Indian families. On arriving at Kittanning,
the two younger children ages 2 and 4 were also taken from her. Lowery's greatest fear was that her children, "the fruit of my body" would
be raised as pagans. Soon after, she was sold as a war prisoner to the
French at Fort Machault on the Allegheny River, north of Kittanning.
Here she gave birth to a girl who lived only a few days. For 14 months
she served, cooking, laundry, and sewing for 50 to 60 soldiers in this
log fort. She reports the opportunity of seeing her children occasionally, perhaps when the Indian families stayed nearby. Lowery was then
transferred as a prisoner to Montreal, a ten-week journey from Machault on foot, horseback, and bateau by way of Lake Erie, Lake Ontario
and the St. Lawrence River. As an orthodox Protestant, a Scots-Irish

TERROR ON THE FRONTIER

Calvinist, she felt pressured and intimidated by the Catholic culture and became assertive about her beliefs. At the end of her servitude in Montreal, she was released to travel as part of a prisoner exchange, first to Quebec, then by ship to England, and finally back to Pennsylvania.

McCullogh's diary fails to note many of the attacks that occurred before mid-August, of which there were approximately nine including the Studebaker attack described above. He does not mention an attack on Fort David Davis in the Little Cove, the Widow Barr attack near Fort McDowell, an attack on Fort McCord and others.

An attack that was recorded stated, "John was killed May ye 26 in yr 1756." With no more information the interpretation is open, though the fact that this entry is written in significantly larger letters suggest its importance to McCullogh. With no last name given, this may mean that this is James's brother John, whom he has mentioned several times in his diary up until this time and never mentions afterward. Therefore, the suggested interpretation is that his brother was killed by the Indians.

The other personal tragedy for McCullogh was the capture of his sons, two months later.

Indian kidnappings were not unknown west of the mountains prior to Braddock's misadventures at Fort Duquesne. In May 1755, 18-year-old James Smith was taken captive while cutting the new wagon road from "Ft Loudon to Turkey Foot or the three forks of the

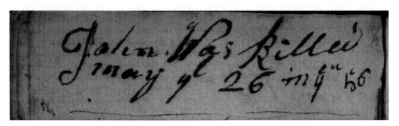

Yohogania." The Indians, three Delawares, had concealed themselves along the road west of Bedford. Smith, who would later make a name for himself as a leader of the Black Boys Rebellion, kept a diary during his years of captivity with the Indians from 1755 to 1759. Apparently the Indian captors had no objection to his keeping these notes in his diary, and one wonders how he was able maintain ink and pen. The whereabouts of the diary is unknown, and it was never published. However, using these notes years later, he personally wrote *An Account of the Remarkable Occurrences in the Life and Travels of Col James Smith, during his captivity with the Indians*, which was published in 1799.

In it, he relates his trip to Fort Duquesne, and the initiation ritual of flogging and beating that he had to endure. Soon after arriving at the fort, he heard the news of Braddock's defeat. James Smith proceeded to describe his travels up the Allegheny River to a town 40 miles north of Fort Duquesne and, three weeks later, to an Indian town on the west branch of the Muskingum, called Tullihas. The description of his treatment and the Indian customs he observed over the years is intriguing.

As mentioned earlier, after Braddock's defeat, Indian kidnappings east of the Appalachians became common as well. One of the first such attacks was in November at Penn's Neck on the Susquehanna River, where 2-year-old Regina Hartman Leininger and sister Barbara were taken captive and eight settlers were killed, including the sisters' father and brother. Barbara was rescued and later married one of her liberators; Regina lived among the Indians for years until she was released following the cessation of hostilities.

On Feb. 11, 1756, near Fort McDowell (on the West Branch three miles north of present-day Mercersburg) John Coxe, his brother, Richard, and John Craig were captured by a band of nine Delaware Indians. On the way to Kittanning, they met Shingas the Terrible on the trail with 30 Delaware warriors, and Captain Jacobs (a Delaware chief whose real name was Tewea, but who had been given the nickname due to his resemblance to a German from Cumberland County) with 15 men heading eastward intending to destroy settlements along the Conococheague.

On reaching the Indian village of Kittanning, the Coxes and John Craig saw about 100 warriors and 50 captives, including men, women and children, many of the captives from Big Cove. Before long, a Delaware party returned with nine scalps and 10 prisoners, and then came another with several scalps and five prisoners. Another company of 18 from Diahogo had seven scalps waving from a pole. The returning warriors then held a council followed by war dances lasting almost a week. The Delaware tribesmen then called all prisoners to watch the torture of one Paul Broadley, who was beaten with clubs and tomahawks, and then fastened to a post so they could chop off his ears and all his fingers. John Coxe shared this description with his fellow frontiersmen after he escaped from his Indian master while on the Susquehanna near Fort Augusta (Sunbury) and returned to the Conococheague. The settlers on the Conococheague came by their fear honestly.

With no governmental protection, local militias did the best they could to rebuff the attacks. In the late summer of 1756, Lt. Col. John Armstrong, whose brother was killed in a raid near Lewistown, took 300 men and headed west over the mountains to Kittanning. Most residents fled, but Captain Jacobs and his family held out in a log cabin, which was set on fire by the colonists. Captain Jacobs escaped the flames, only to be killed and scalped, a handsome bounty having been placed on his head by colonial governments. But while Armstrong was hailed as the "Hero of Kittanning," the short-term effect of the raid was to rile up the Delaware, who in the name of revenge stepped up their attacks.

That following summer, Indian hostilities visited the McCullogh family. The attacks up and down the frontier had escalated severely. From the time of Braddock's defeat through March of the following year, the French estimated that Indians killed 700 colonists from Pennsylvania through North Carolina. This was why James decided to take his family away from the dangerous frontier back east across the Cumberland Valley to the Antietam Creek settlement on the Maryland/Pennsylvania border. Three months later, in order to tend his crops, he moved his family back to the Conococheague settlement near the Great Valley Trail, not far to the northeast from Cross's Fort. They were staying in a small cabin next to the Great Road in an area that seemed to be relatively safe. This was south of Pawling's Tavern on the Great Road. From there, James could travel five miles north to work on his farm while leaving his family at this fort or safe house.

The events of July 26, 1756, receive a brief notation in James McCullogh's diary—"John and James mcColoch Was taken Captive by ye indins from Canogogige, July ye 26 1756." There is no mention of either son afterward in the diary. Perhaps too much grief was present, or maybe it was the custom in colonial times not to dwell on feelings. Maybe he expressed his perseverance in this later entry: "O greatly

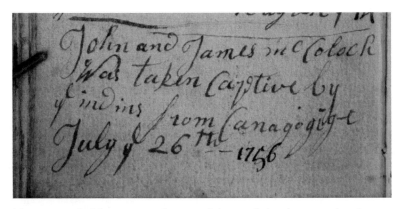

blest o greatly blest ye people yt joyful sound that know in brightness of thy face o Lord they ever on shall go."

A detailed account of the kidnapping was handed down by his son John in a work entitled *Life With the Aborigines.* According to John's narrative, on the fateful day his parents and older sister had gone to up to the farm to harvest flax, accompanied by John Allen, a friend from Fort Loudon. John Allen had started home when he heard that the Indians had killed a man that morning about one and a half miles from the McCullogh farm.

Allen then took a circuitous route of six to seven miles back to the McCullogh safe house where John and James were playing. Allen told them to go immediately into the house to be safe. But "people were in a bustle preparing to go to Cross's Fort, and discussing who should give the McCullogh parents notice." Unfortunately, none would venture to go, so the two sons, ages 8 and 5, took it upon themselves to journey up to the farm in order to warn their father that dangerous Indians were in the area. The boys took off their trousers and kept their shirts on and left unnoticed by anyone, leaving their two-year-old sister Mary sleeping in a bed.

When the boys had reached the border of the farm, within 50 or 60 yards of the house, they "began to halloo and sing" to warn their parents. All of a sudden, they were captured by five Indians and one Frenchman, who divided into two parties, with three in front of the boys and three behind. This part seemed "more like a dream than anything real; my brother screamed aloud the instant we saw them." They first seized John by his shirt, and then chased after James, who was trying to run up the hill to the house. The Indians ran up to get their baggage, where they pulled out a pair of moccasins that they tied onto John's feet.

The Indians then started off as fast as John could run with them; one of the Indians carried the brother, James, on his back. They ran along the side of the field where the parents were working, but were out of view because of a small ridge in the field. They travelled eastward to Back Run, then followed it north to St Thomas. They next went to a rendezvous point behind Mt. Parnell where Edenville is today. They crossed the mountain into Bear Valley and then into Horse Valley. The Indians then took their captives across the mountains into Path Valley and camped along a stream (the west branch of the Conococheague Creek). This route passed through unpopulated areas.

The journey to the Allegheny River can be traced on a map of the Allegheny Mountain and plateaus. At an Indian town near Fort Duquesne, John was bathed in the Allegheny River. On arrival at Fort Duquesne, John says they were taken to a Frenchman's house not far from the fort where an Indian chief took James Jr. by the hand and offered him to another Frenchman. The younger James was given to the Frenchman—whether a trader or a missionary is unknown—and was never heard from again.

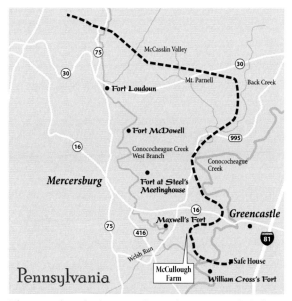

The route by which sons John and James traveled, from the safe house to home, and then the route taken by the Indians who held them captive.

In John's narrative, he says he was taken to Shenango on the Ohio River in present day Mercer County where he lived for two and a half years with the Indians. He tells of being taken to towns near Venango, up the Allegheny River—one town was called Mohoning and another Kseek-he-oong, or Salt Licks. It seem that a trader from Shippensburg by the name of Andrew Wilkins came to Salt Licks in 1759 and started asking John where he was from and his name. John said he was from Cononocheague and that his name was McCullogh. As soon as the trader returned to Shippensburg, he informed James senior that he had seen his son.

Sometime during the following summer, James McCullogh crossed the mountains and found John in a nearby town of Mohoning.

John was shy in speaking with his father, even through an interpreter. His father left and returned to Pittsburgh. The following fall, James went out to Fort Venango or French Creek along with Wilkins. There is the undated balance sheet of "an account of charges laid out during our travel to ye Back Country." Although James McCullogh does not elaborate on this in his diary, John supplies information in his narrative written years later. Note that James, the father, was no longer maintaining diary entries after 1758.

At this meeting, James offered to purchase his son, effectively paying a ransom. An Indian brother negotiated and agreed, but John wept at the thought of leaving his Indian family. On the way back to Conococheague, he refused to stay on a horse. The first night, about midnight, John ran off and hid in a tree to escape. John was finally returned to his family by Gen. Henry Bouquet after the war.

Many of the Indian attacks that took place between 1755 and 1758 in this region were recorded by James McCullogh in the diary. Following the capture of his two sons, his diary entries include almost all the hostilities.

In the year 1757, the attacks increased in number and extended over a wider area. In the diary he records 36, from local ones to a quarry at Fort Frederick in Maryland, to Shimokin, to Harris's Ferry (Harrisburg), to Biggers Gap, and Opecan (Opequon) Creek, Va., among others. The first 1757 attack was recorded on March 27 at Rocky Springs near Chambersburg, Pa., where "one woman (was) killed and all carried away captive."

Next, on April 2, "near cursell Chambers (Cornell Chambers) Fort ... Willem MCKinly" and his son killed." The same day another attack that wasn't recorded in the diary occurred at Back Creek near

Chambersburg, when were 11 members of three families were killed, and some were taken prisoner. The next diary entry records an attack on April 17 near the Potomac River, noting that Jeremiah Jack was captured and two of his sons killed, while one man and a woman drowned trying to escape.

The same year, McCullogh noted in his diary that his family "moved to ye cabin at Willem McCrereies May ye 19 1757." His diary continues to record a string of attacks, scalping and captive taking on the frontier. Some were nearby, such this one at Fort Maxwell less than two miles away: "Apriel 23 John Marlen and Willem blear was killed and Patrick McCleland wounded near Maxwells the year 1757." And he includes reports from further away along the Potomac River: "May ye 4 Mager Cambel and tussy was killed or carried away captives with 14 other persons near potomock."

In 1758, McCullogh records eight attacks in his diary, the last on July 20 at "Seatara," which may refer to Swatara, a creek in the Harrisburg area. But two other notable attacks occurred. One was the attack on the Jemison home in Buchanan Valley west of Gettysburg, where Mary Jemison was taken captive, and the other was in Path Valley up the Conocheague Creek where Hugh Mercer went in pursuit of the Indians after two persons were killed.

Those who were captured through the years experienced a variety of fates. The captives under the command of the Delaware warriors were taken west across the Allegheny Mountain ranges on a well-established Franktown-Logstown trail that led from the upper reaches of the west branch of the Conococheague Creek to the Indian settlement Kittanning on the Allegheny River, an important staging area for Indian attacks. This was a distance of more than 100 miles. The Indian parties kept up a brisk, nonstop pace during the day, and sometimes at night too, without food for the first day, with bare feet at times or moccasins that offered little protection over steep, rocky paths. The route passed over streams and through thicket and briars. The Indians pushed their captives relentlessly with the intent of escaping any rescue party that might be chasing them.

Depending on the location of capture, the Indians sought inconspicuous routes to reach the trail in Path Valley. One route wound its way across the mountains from Fort McCord west across the mountains and the upper Conodoguinet Creek in order to reach the west branch of the Conococheague Creek to avoid detection by frontier sentinels. From the Upton area the captives were taken through the thickets of Back Creek to the east in order to circumvent more inhabited areas. From Fort McDowell, the route was more direct, going north and passing to the west of Parnell Knob into Path Valley.

Cruelty was one aspect of the Indian personality. But as cruel as they were in war, when they took captives with the purpose of adopting them, they treated them, as C. Hale Sipe says in The Indian Chiefs of Pennsylvania, "as their own flesh and blood, instead of enslaving them. Tribes were attempting to rebuild their numbers following the devastation of prior epidemics all the way back to the 1600s. Women and children were treated with a kindness and respect often found lacking among the whites." This might explain the reluctance of some captives to return home. And no white woman, adopted by the Indians, needed to fear the violation of her honor.

The tide of violence began to turn in late October 1758, with the Treaty of Easton (signed in Easton, Pa.) in which more than a dozen tribes including the Delaware and Shawnee, agreed to drop their alliance with the French. In exchange, the British recognized the Indians' rights to land west of the Appalachians. Two years later, the British captured Montreal, effectively ending the Seven Years War in the North American theatre. The war itself ended in 1763, but ensuing British bullying and controversial tactics led to a rekindling of Indian hostilities in a rebellion known as Pontiac's War. The British at Ft. Pitt tried to engage in biological warfare by giving smallpox-infected blankets into Indian camps, but the Indians had already been exposed and were ill.

CHAPTER 7

Return to the Textile Business

As the war and Indian violence wound down, McCullogh was able to return to farming and his business of producing linen out of flax. Flax is one of the oldest fiber crops in the world, having been cultivated for at least 5,000 years. And dyed fibers from wild flax were found in the Dzudzuana Cave in the Republic of Georgia dating back 30,000 years. As a weaver by trade, flax would have been James McCullogh's cash cow.

For McCullogh to take up the linen trade in the New World as efficiently as he did, he must have had significant knowledge and experience from his earlier years before migrating from Northern Ireland. In his diary he refers to quite a variety of fabrics and textile products. They are lincey, linen (or linin), lining, tikin, hikrey, sheatin, bagin, lincey striped, shirtin, stript, cloth covering, girthin, tow, wolling or woling chack, stroud and green cloth.

The following list summarizes the types of products James Mc-Cullogh paid employees to make. One would imagine that his wife, Martha, and other family members contributed additional production. Note that some of the linen products were made only sporadically.

Fabric Terms mentioned in James McCullogh's book

lincey linen (or ***linin***). This probably refers to "linsey-woolsey," a blend of linen and wool, with a linen warp and a woolen weft.

lining This may refer to a particular fabric for lining or a spelling of linen.

tikin (ticking) A linen twill used to enclose feathers in mattresses and pillows.

hikrey Hickory cloth was a coarse cotton twill similar to denim, longwearing and usually used for work clothes.

sheatin (sheeting) was a type of linen, slightly coarser than a normal shirt linen but not as coarse as tow.

bagin was a coarse weave for making bags.

lincey striped This was an inexpensive striped linsey-woolsey, often used to clothe slaves or indentured servants.

shirtin (shirting) This is a more finely woven fabric used for men's shirts.

stript Probably McCullogh's spelling of "striped."

girthin A coarse weave, strong and interwoven used for saddle girths.

tow was made from the short flax fibers utilized in a very coarse plain weave, usually used for sacks and wrapping cloths, and sometimes men's clothing.

wolling or ***woling chack*** This may mean "woolen" "woolen check."

stroud A course woolen cloth or blanket.

green cloth A finer and more expensive fabric, as the color green was not easy to achieve.

Clothing in colonial days was made of either linen or wool. On the frontier, the linen would have been called homespun, which differentiated it from higher quality imports. Cotton was still a rarity limited to wealthy merchants of Philadelphia or Virginia. Deerskin was used for outer garments and leggings. For linen, smaller or even peasant farmers generally grew the flax, often as a side crop. But McCullogh must have grown flax in some sizable quantities. Irish flax was known to be particularly strong, and better than that grown in other European countries such as Russia and Holland.

Flax grown for fiber or for seed is of the same family (*linum usitatissimum*), but each has different habits of growth. For flax fiber, the seed is sown thickly, in a close stand, so that the plant grows slender and tall, up to four feet in height. When the flax had grown several inches, all weeds were pulled by hand to rid the crop of weeds that that could seriously degrade the quality of the flax fiber.

Where linseed is the objective, such as grown for future plantings, flax is sown thinly so it can branch out to have a maximum yield of seed. Flax seed may be brown or golden in color. A process called rippling removes the seeds, where small bundles of dried flax are pulled through a metal comb, which saves the seeds for making flaxseed oil. Both the short-stemmed and the long-stemmed flax fiber can be used to produce the vegetable oil known as flaxseed or linseed oil (high in omega-3 fatty acids). The seeds are stable while whole, but must be broken down by chewing or grinding for digestive absorption. Linseed oil was used in the manufacture of paints and as a water repellant.

According to his diary, some of the times McCullogh planted flax were March 31, 1750, June 28, 1750 and July 11, 1750. Then he planted on March 20, 1751, April 28, 1758 and March 20-29, 1759.

Planting earlier in the year facilitates the processing of the fiber for linen, as the "retting" (or rotting) process needs to be done in hot weather.

The plants are pulled out by the root, not cut. They were dried by placing tied bundles against a fence in a sunny location. McCullogh records that he threshed flax July 12, 1750, and July 19, 1751, which may refer to harvesting the flaxseed. This is usually done about 30 days after the flax has bloomed. The flax is allowed to dry out and the seedpods are cut off. In colonial days, the retting was often done by throwing the cut and dried stems into a pond or a tub or any water that would be fairly warm. Retting is a process of fermentation by bacterial species such as Clostridia or retting fungi. This process breaks down the hard shell surrounding the fiber to enable that it be removed. After the retting, the stems are again dried. Then the stems are passed through a flax-break, which crumbles the woody shell around the fiber. The shell fragments, called shives, are then removed by scraping them off with a wooden tool called a skutch, which looks like a paddle. Then what remains can be removed by pulling the fibers through a set of long, iron nails, called hackels. This cleans off any remaining particles of the stem shell and also combs the fibers out straight. Now the fibers are ready for spinning into thread, and are wrapped on a winder for later use in the making of linen fabrics. With so many steps, it is clear that past experience in preparing flax fiber would be indispensible.

James McCullogh could have raised the flax by himself, but the production of the linen goods would have been a more labor-intensive operation for which he would have had to employ the help of others. Among those employed were other family members, and in fact, families acted much like small businesses.

How Flax is Made

Flax

Full
Dry
Riffle

Retting → Dry → Flax Brake

Scutching Board and Knife

Niddy Noddy

Hackle

Flax Wheel

Occasionally Dyed

Occasionally Dyed

Quill and Screen Winder

Shuttle

Scarne

Wash and Bleach

Warping Frame

Linen

emotional blow, but it also would have been an economic blow because as the boys grew older their labor would have been counted upon in the family/company. McCullogh's other children, other than Jean born in 1746, would not have been old enough early on for meaningful work so McCullogh would have hired journeymen or relied on his siblings. One was his older brother Archibald, mentioned frequently in the diary. Another was Sara, his sister, whom he lists as Sara McCullogh as apparently she was unmarried. And then there is a John, whose last name is not revealed, and is assumed to be his brother as the last name is mentioned with "John" in other places in the diary. John was said to be a little older, which would have placed him between Archibald, born in 1715, and James, who was born about 1721. John's name shows up frequently in the early years until an entry recording John's death at the hands of the Indians in March 1756. No other record has been found to document this, so it is not known where this happened or how.

Some entries involving his family members and the linen trade include:

— In 1748, "14 pence to John McCullogh opon Saras account and 13 yeards of shirting…"

— In September 1750, "detor to Archibald McCullogh in balance 0.9s. 7 pence." "Archibald McCullogh to amatick (?) 3 s 2 pence and to a bel (belt orbell) 1 and a walat (wallet)1-6 and 6 pence…"

Throughout, Archibald and Sara were regular purchasers of linen from James.

Before 1753, the names of some customers mentioned in the diary are Mathew Patons, John McCullogh, James Prier, James John Creadit, Sara McCullogh, Willem Carson, Mrs James, Samul Killpatrick,

James John and John Wats, and others.

After 1753, the ledger included: John Robison, Charity Courtney, Adam Armstrong, Archibald McColoch, John Woods, Samul torintine, Ephraim Smith, Colin Spence, Cormick Derman, Peter Krall, Tomas Devison, Joseph Willson, Willem McCreary, Robert McCay (McCoy), Ganel Gavis, plus others. Some sample entries give an idea of his productivity:

Entries from April to June 1755:

Colin Spence 60 yds of linen woven in march 55	30
& 17 yds of baging in Apriel	7
& 10 yeards of covering	10
&1 bushel of flax seed	4
& 2 yeards if girthing 1	21
and 25 yeards of linen Jun	126
19 yeards of hikrey in may	L1-1-8
18 yeards of lincey	9

Also,

"John Woods to 22 yeards of lincey woven Jeneway ye 21st 1756 more to 41 yeards of girth web feberwary ye 29th"

"December ye 15 Robert McCay to 15 yeards of linen and woling chack woven 1759" and "Robert McCay to 18 yeards of blankets wover Janeway ye 8 1760."

His linen customers after moving to Upton included: Mary Kelley, David Anderson, David Ralston, Widow Routey, Patrick McIntire, David Stoner (the brother of an ancestor of the Charles J. Stoner, who helped work on this diary for the Franklin County Historical Society), Willem Baxter (paid Dec 20, 1758 with one bushel of corn),

Colin Spence, Willem McCreary, David Maxel, Joshua Homes and others. Some sample entries:

— "Jenuary ye 10th 1753 John Robison to 37 yeards of lining woven £ 0-15-5." (Note: 0-15-5 indicates pounds-shillings-pence).

— "Jun ye 10th (1753) Mary Kelley to 5 yeards of tikin 0-2-6 & in cash lent 0-3-6 at Chisteen for rum and onye 18 of Agust 0-2-0 in lent to hugh" (possibly Hugh Kelly?).

— "Patrick McIntire to 24 yeards of linen woven September ye 23 1755" followed by "Received from patrick mctire five shillings said day."

Note the paucity of German names, suggesting they were not nearby. In addition, the list of customers does not seem to include many of his neighbors and others in the area. For example, there is no entry that he sold fabrics to the Rev. John Steel or the physician Hugh Mercer, who lived in a house over a spring a mile west of Upton. There are many reasons to suspect the diary is only a partial record, but there could be other, less obvious reasons. Maybe he was generous and made donations, or maybe a lot of his fabrics were sold by bartering and not listed in the diary.

At this time, the British had a colonial policy expecting the new colonies or territories to produce raw material to be shipped to England for the process of manufacturing. This supported British business as the manufactured goods were not only sold in England, but also exported by British merchants for sale through stores throughout the colonies. Steel and Mercer, as well as others who do not appear as customers in the diary, most likely traveled to cities such as Philadelphia, preferring the finer British fabrics to the homemade ones on the frontier. The simple loom that James McCullogh had brought to the

frontier would not have produced the fine fabrics that more sophisti-
cated looms did.

The chart on the following page shows the voume of McCullogh's
production.

Volume of Product Produced & Sold by McCullough and His Employees

	1750	1751	1752	1753	1754	1755	1756	1757	1758
Linin (*linen, plain*)	40		5			63	187	63	54
Lincey	37	9	84		36	24	24		
Shirting		66	97		5				
Striped	3		13½						
Ticking	40								
Hikrey	41	15	15						
Girthing	32			41	21				
Tow					20				
Woolen			30		37	11			
Blankets	6				21			18	

CHAPTER 8

Religion's Central Role in McCullogh's Life

It's often stated that the Ulster Presbyterians left Ireland for the New World in "waves;" indeed they did, and there's a practical reason for that. Among the qualities that made Ireland desirable to the Scots in the first place was an abundance of land and stable leases that were 31 years in duration. Large groups of Scots entered into these contracts at a time and, when they were up, these "waves" of Scots-Irish generally decided to move on instead of renewing.

But religion would have been another driving force for immigration as ecclesiastical minorities were increasingly treated legally as second-class citizens. Presbyterian ministers led the charge for migration, scouting out new turf across the Atlantic and eagerly reporting back to the congregations. In the colonies, you could own your own good land and worship as you pleased. The Scots-Irish didn't leave in a trickle; they left thousands at a time.

The Presbyterian Church followed the migrations to this expanding frontier by providing ministers who supplied the series of Presbyterian "meetings," as churches were called. Official recognition of this expansion took place with the formation in 1732 of the Presbytery of Donegal, the first Presbytery formed in the area (the first presbytery in America was the Presbytery of Philadelphia, organized in 1705). The original territory of the Presbytery of Donegal was Lancaster County in Pennsylvania and it extended "as far west as settlers cared to go."

The minutes of this presbytery abound with requests for ministerial supplies and assignments of the presbytery to meet these demands. With all the distress that befell the frontier settlers at the time of the French and Indian War, the Presbyterian church sought to alleviate the suffering and distress through a relief agency the "Corporation for the Relief of Poor and distressed Presbyterian Ministers, and of the poor and Distressed Widows and Children of Presbyterian Ministers." The agency was incorporated in the colony of Pennsylvania in 1759.

After coming to America as a teen with his mother and other immigrants, Charles Beatty (whose diary has previously been mentioned) studied with the evangelist William Tennant at Neshaminy (in what is present-day Bucks County) during the course of his education. It was Tennant who persuaded Beatty to enter the ministry. Beatty completed his ministerial studies, was licensed "for preaching the everlasting Gospel," and installed over the congregation at Neshaminy where he remained as pastor until his death in 1772. But his ministerial duties required much travel. In 1760 he was chosen to visit England to solicit funds for the Corporation under the general assembly of the Church of Scotland where he—albeit with the caveat of Indian terrors—continued to inspire New World recruits. He visited Scotland and the North of Ireland, preaching seven or eight times in each country soliciting support.

It is likely that James McCullogh heard Beatty preach on one of the activist preacher's trips to the frontier, including Beatty's stint as army chaplain during the French & Indian war. Contemporary minutes of Donegal Presbytery state that Beatty and Reverend George Duffield, pastor of the Presbyterian Church at Carlisle, who traveled with Beatty in 1766 "found on the frontier numbers of people, earnestly desirous of forming themselves into congregations, and declaring their willingness to exert their utmost order to have the gospel among them, but in circumstances exceedingly necessitous from the late calamities of war in these parts." James McCullogh would have been among that "number of people."

He records in his diary that he carried three books to the new world: his Bible, Watson's *Body of Divinity* and Brown's *Explanation of the Romans.*

On the frontier, James McCullogh kept his Bible at the ready for the obvious reason that religion was one of the primary reasons he had settled in the middle of a land that was beautiful and productive, but also lonely and violent. When the work seemed insurmountable and the dangers too great, the Bible would remind him that there was no one who could deny him his faith—except, perhaps for other Presbyterians, seeing as how there were many dissenters within the dissenters, and many arguments about the one true path to salvation.

But for McCullogh, the Bible was more than that. The Bible was his guide through life, the scriptures his interpreter of events that he could not otherwise understand. In his diary, McCullogh let the Bible do the talking when words failed him. On moving to his new farm at Conococheague, he cited Psalms 89:15, "O greatly blest o greatly blest ye people ye joyful sound that know in brightness of thy face o Lord they even on shall go." In a note on the birth of his son, he noted the size and potential of the Red Sea, which "is 15 mils broad and 5 fathoms deep."

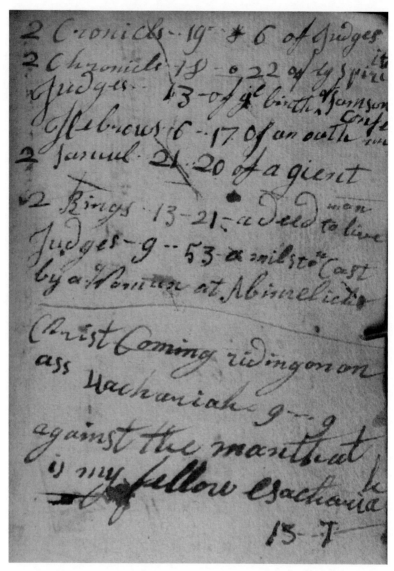

The Bible was James McCullogh's guide for his life. Scriptures such as these noted here helped him interpret events that he might not otherwise understand.

The interpretation of McCullogh's chosen verses is mostly a matter of conjecture since he seldom expands upon them. One verse hints at a betrayal—perhaps focused on an employee? Another recounts the triumph of the master riding into town on a donkey, maybe at a time that he is feeling vindicated? Elsewhere he quotes Judges, "a woman dropped an upper millstone on his head and cracked his skull." One hesitates to even guess.

The entries do create an image of a man and a religion finding their way together. As he sailed to America and even through the kidnapping of his sons, McCullogh was still a relatively young man, not yet 40 years of age. Much of what he had experienced to this point would have seemed overwhelming.

The Ulster Presbyterians had proudly born the mantel of "dissenter" in old England, but gradually this moniker fell by the wayside because, strictly speaking, in the colonial mixing bowl of religions there was nothing to dissent from. There was no more tithing, no more laws penalizing those whose religions were out of the mainstream. For every new group that stepped off of the ship, there was a new religion that came along with them.

On the frontier, lines became blurred. In a land of few churches, beggars could not be choosers and Scots-Irish might end up under the same meetinghouse roof as Welsh or Germans, assuming, of course, that on the rough-and-tumble frontier they subscribed to religion at all. In Conococheague, there is evidence of divided churches, possibly because, in a reaction to a violent, profane, hard-drinking frontier, some congregations reverted to the same strict, hard-core rules that they had thrown off back home.

The frontier church served as a hub of authority and public safety. Many churches were modified into fortresses when Indians threatened the region. Ministers dispensed justice and led war parties—they would later become officers in the American Revolution—consistent with a religion that had come to the New World seeking to cast off the yoke of authority.

In 1755, following the defeat of General Braddock, McCullogh's friend, the Rev. John Steel fortified his Church Hill meetinghouse with a palisade as protection from Indian raids, but even so, the disruption of these repeated raids caused families to scatter, and the congregation for a while was disbanded. During this time, Rev. Steel carried his rifle with him to places of worship and had it by his side as he preached. Once, as he conducted a service in Greencastle he was informed of a raid on a Walters family at Rankins Mill on Muddy Run, about a mile from Greencastle. The minister stopped the service, took his rifle in hand, and gathered a group of riflemen together in pursuit of the attackers.

Steel was notified in March 1756 that he had been appointed captain of a company in the pay of the province and that he was to be posted at McDowell's Mill (Fort McDowell) along Forbes Road. Companies of 13 men were formed under James Burd, Hance Hamilton, James Patterson and High Mercer. Later in 1756, the Rev./Capt. Steel's company was in the expedition under Armstrong against Kittanning.

In 1758, the Church Hill meetinghouse burned and the Rev. Steel left the frontier for Carlisle, where he served until 1776.

For McCullogh, as for the frontier, religion was a focal point of life. His diary reflects this, as his religion is pervasive throughout all aspects of his life. It might also demonstrate that—although his diary is devoid of personal emotion—he was not a man without feeling. He had not mentioned the birth of his daughter Jean, but when she "did enter to John Robison scol..." he quoted Psalms, "O that men ye lord would give prais for his goodness ... & for his works of wonder done unto ye sons on men."

Perhaps this was the pride of a tough Scots-Irishman showing through.

CHAPTER 9

McCullogh the Businessman

On the frontier, settlers were self-sustaining; they had to make what they used—clothes, tools, furniture, cleaning products. The diary indicates that James McCullogh purchased only a few items from time to time for his family's provision. In 1748, as he was settling into his new farm at Marsh Creek south of Gettysburg, he paid James John two pounds, four shillings for a hog. He continued to buy hogs through most of his time at Marsh Creek.

In 1748 he also purchased corn. Later, he purchased molasses several times as in 1751, 1753 and 1754 ("15 pence to thomas Montgomery Apriel 1 for molasses"). McCullogh bought butter for his family in 1752 and 1753.

In October 1750 (or perhaps 1756?) there were some other items "an account of goods from thomas Montgomery," including:

— two ys and 3 quarters of chapes (cloak?)   9-2

— 2 handcurchees   5

— and ditto cotton   3-0

— one wisted cap   2-4

— 1 half yeard of linin and one quarter and A half of ... camrick 0-3-9

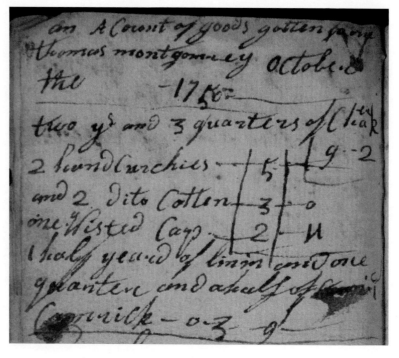

And we see in 1752,

"November 26 to one new testament" 2-4

— one quarter yeard of green cloth   1-3p

Generally speaking, he bought those things he could not make himself, so this last notation of the purchase of cloth is puzzling as he was in the weaving business and "linen" is noted in the previous page; it suggests he was unable to make this type of cloth. Perhaps McCullogh was preoccupied in 1752 by the purchase of his new farm in Conococheague. Next we see, on "October ye 5 1752 Willem imer to one cow hide 42 pounds mor to two, hide 45 pounds." Also on Oct. 5, McCullogh bought 22.5 pounds of butter.

In 1754, on his new farm at Upton, (which perhaps was not yet up to full operation) he "received one bushel & one half of wheat by Daniel Gilmer and one bushel ditto July ye 10th James McCologh" and on the next line, "[   ] bushels of wheat in September to 10 yeards of blankets in October." Apparently, he was being paid in wheat for the textiles he provided.

These entries no doubt made perfect sense to McCullogh at the time, but are confounding to modern readers.

He also makes note of services he received and mentions other items of machinery and equipment.

An entry of 1749 reads, "A memorandum of Smith (blacksmith) work between Arter Lockert and me in year 1749 and first krak (crack) to a little pot of my own irn (iron) on couter 12 pounds weight and on [ ] to a two hors (horse) tree of my irn and on ring to joyn frisens. Of my irn and one kepel to tree of my ikrn & two plow pleats of my iron & on (one) cleavish welded led a [   ] onst lead and mend the shoulder one day one hour 3 shillings and a shir (sheer) onst sharped and a coulter twice sharped."

This was ironwork, first to a patch a crack in a little pot, and then to add a 12-pound counterweight to a plow coulter plate. He needed work on a two-horse tree (the pivoting crossbar that joins draft animals to a wagon or plow) probably for a two-horse plow; one ring to join something else on the tree; and two plow pleats of iron (used to repair plows).

In 1755, when there was fear of Indian attacks, the diary entries mentioned an interesting list of tools he hid to keep them from being stolen:

"I did hide wolingers (winnowers) and some shafts in a halou (hallow) tree upon ye top of ye hill above ye garden ... and a pitch fork and gers (gears) and pulley stocks above ye barn amongst ye wheat ... and a gurne and salt under upper berrech (barrack) next ye cow recks (racks) ... and a great deal of other youtencils in a gurne (this seems to be some sort of cart) in the head of a prato furr below ye stable ... and a plow shear and cleaves in a tree or lag (log) before ye calf house door within ye field." He seems to have hidden his valuable farm tools, those most difficult to replace.

It should be noted that this entry gives some idea about his farm buildings in 1755, two years after he moved to Upton. He notes a barn with wheat, upper hay barracks, a calf house, a stable and cow racks.

Undated entry on 57B mentions more routine maintenance:

— " a shir sharpened 0-4-9 and mended 4-1-3

— two plou pleats 0-1-6

— a shir and coulter (plow blade) twice sharped 0-1-9 0-8-0"

The farm-equipment repairs were probably basic, but one would still expect him to mention attention paid to more equipment, such as the loom needed for weaving. It is likely that he had a homemade loom as the bigger looms would have been too big to transport.

Along with equipment expenses, the diary accounts for land leases, including the notation, "decmbr 6th 1758 rec'c of james MCollock one pound five shillings it being in part one year rent. I sat recd by mee Henry Black." This can be assumed to be nearby land. Tax records for Peters Township list a James Black in 1753.

Another expense on the farm would have been labor, at least until the children were old enough to work on their own. McCullogh mentions his help's timesheets, including "September 11 1753 James

Linsey got one month in November and December & a ... week & ye 2 week in Jeneway in full and 4 days and ye 4 week in full ye first week in febery 1 day and 30 days at scoll and 17 days at his own hand & one day of Charity Courtney"

Charity Courtney shows up a number of times as a paid worker, and there is some insight into what these employees did: "June 29 1754 John Woods to 15 yeards of baging mor (more meaning also) to 16 yeards of to (tow) cloath & one day & a half reaping & one dozen of yearn spinning." This shows that this helper did weaving, reaping and spinning.

Given the amount of work that had to be done, he must have had considerable help either from this family or other employees that were not entered into the diary.

Taken as a whole, these entries paint the picture of a small businessman, dealing with small and not-so-small details of entrepreneurship. But along with running a textile business, James McCullogh conducted financial transactions with a number of people over the years, beginning soon after his arrival in 1747. These are in addition to accounts carried in his book for items that he had sold. First in 1747, "I did give James Johns (the man from whom he purchased his pork) money and Moris willems money to beckey Reed," and then, "I did get twenty shillings from morgan John and I did give said money to Lorans McSorley." Then, "May ye 15th Dened McFall to shillings & 9 pence in cash lent your not to go..." Later, on November 23, "to 20 shillings in cash lent to Willem Tomson." That is followed by, "Jan 21, 1753 Willem Tomson to 20 shillings in cash lent Agust ye 17 to 10 yeards of shirtin woven."

It is interesting that he records, "December ye 30 1757 Samul Gettey to 15 shilling in cash lent by me James McColoch." A Samuel Gettys opened a tavern in south-central Pennsylvania in 1761, and his son James laid out the town of Gettysburg. But this financial transaction is dated in the time that McCullogh was in Upton, having left the Gettysburg area several years earlier so it may be a different person.

In February and March 1758, McCullogh was lending a few shillings in cash to Maren Love, William Moore and James Gouley. These loans in 1758 could have been a time of hardship for many as a result of the French and Indian War.

A fastidious bookkeeper at times, James McCollogh also kept account of his travel expenses when trying to ransom his sons from the Indians, in "an account of charges laid out during our travel to y Back Country £1-3-3."

McCullogh's financial transactions are curious for a couple of reasons. First, the Scots-Irish as a rule did not arrive in New Castle with extra spending money. Indeed, one of the primary complaints about the Ulster Scots was their habit of squatting on any piece of property available, lacking the funds for a more acceptable acquisition of real estate. Second, the frontier in the mid-1700s was largely a barter society, with little available cash of any kind. James McCullogh's rightfully purchased property and financial transactions would indicate that he was fortunate enough to arrive in the New World with money, and was able to make more once he was here.

CHAPTER 10

Writing in Code

Of all the curiosities of James McCullogh's diary, none is more mystifying than his disposition to, on occasion, write in code. Writing in code was not entirely unknown in colonial America. The larger-than-life Virginia plantation owner William Byrd II encoded his diary, a cipher that was not cracked until 1939. Byrd certainly had some experiences—such as kissing slave girls and the time he "kissed an felt" the hotel maid—that could have caused some embarrassment had the general public been privy to them at the time.

McCullogh's coded entries by contrast concern subject matter that is relatively tame and would hardly need to be kept secret. And even beyond that, it was a moot point since McCullogh provided the key to his code in the pages of his book. Here's one for the reader to decode:

On page 6 of the diary, dated 1748, is found "79c266 hd5 a 62tt29s EC 48 the 48 side 38 th3s fish 8282a9 745th" What does that mean?

This entry was presumably made after he has settled in his property at Little's Run in Mt. Joy Township and was not just passing time on his voyage across the Atlantic, but why use the code?

Farther into the diary this entry appears with the information for deciphering the code:

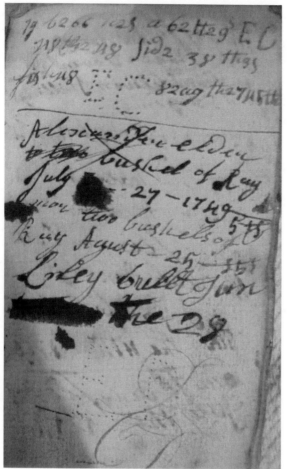

Page 6 of the diary.

With this key, "3172s 7cC464gh," reads "James McCollogh" and "h3s h18d 18d ye 28 38 h4p2" (his hand and ye (p)en in hope).

Note that there was no "j" in McCullogh's code alphabet. Instead of James, he would have written "iames." In eighteenth and early nineteenth century conventions, the letter "I" was substituted for "J."

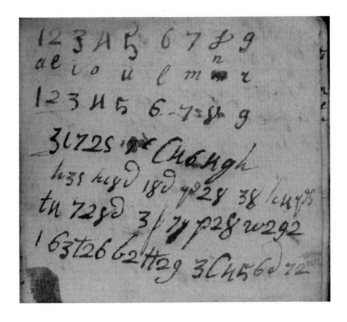

```
1 2 3 4 5 6 7 8 9
a e i o u l m n r
1 2 3 4 5 6 7 8 9
```

One can only wonder what was motivating James McCullogh. Was there a goal or purpose? Could this have been a diversion or entertainment? Or was he planning on using it for keeping veiled entries in this book? The decoding of the first 1746 entry reads: "Mr cell has a letters CC – On the on(e) side in this fash(i)on near the mouth." Again, the reader may guess as to the meaning here—a scar or a tattoo? As these entries are dated the year he came to America, was this a way to pass time on the boat?

The next entries chronologically were entered when he had settled on his new farm in Upton (p17B): "b56t 38 ye y219," which translates to "Built in ye 1753," which must refer to one of the new buildings on his new farm.

In the next year, 1754, we find: "7y ch392y t4k b566 Ju6y ye 14 1754," which reads "my Chirey tok bull, July 14, 1754."

Then appear two entries from 1757 on page 48B: "July ye 1ˢᵗ I did plow corn at W36627 7c C292s." (I did plow corn at Willem McCreres').

Next on page 56B is: "st21t62y t4k b566 Jul ye 16 57" ('Steatley tok bull July ye 16, 1757'.)

With these last two entries on cows encountering a bull, was there some issue that needed secrecy? At least one author has speculated that he might have acquired the services of the bull without compensation and did not want to advertise the fact.

These coded entries add an intriguing aspect to the diary, and in some ways are emblematic of the text as a whole, with its many mysteries.

Postscript

The pages of James McCullogh's diary were filled for the most part by 1758 and there are no entries after 1760, when McCullogh was about 40 years old. He would live for another two decades, suggesting the possibility of a second volume that has been lost, though one would have expected such another volume would be listed in his estate after his passing.

One event that would have been interesting to know about from McCullogh's perspective would have been the Pontiac's War attack on the Enoch Brown school house between Williamson and Greencastle on July 26 1764. James's brother Archibald had enrolled his young son in the school that was attacked by four Delaware Indians in what became one of the last but most hideous acts of violence in Conococheague. Enoch Brown, the schoolmaster was killed and scalped after pleading for the lives of his students. The Indians then turned on the class, tomahawking and scalping the students, killing nine and taking four as prisoners. Two of the children who were scalped survived, including Archie, who suffered brain damage in the attack. The Indians returned from their rampage—the day before they had beaten a pregnant woman to death and cut the fetus from her body—to their village in the Ohio Territory where James' son John was still captive. John later wrote that the marauders where browbeaten by the chiefs as cowards for taking the scalps of children.

Sometime between 1757 and the return of his son John in 1764, James relocated to a new and larger farm property near to Church Hill. Again, it is puzzling that there is no mention of the move in the diary, even though one would suspect that it was before 1760. McCullogh maintained his linen business on this farm, which was bordered on the farms of two friends, John McClellan to the south and George Galbraith to the east. His title to this land was recorded in 1771.

The frontier was changing dramatically during these years leading up to his death in 1781. Roads were being improved, and a major development would have been wagon-accessible routes to eastern markets in Baltimore and Philadelphia.

McCullogh's will was dated May 2, 1778, and "Proved" (probated) March 15, 1786. A young heifer was willed to each of his daughters Jean McClellan and Mary Foster, and one to brother Archibald Mc-Cullough as well as to grandson, James McClellan and granddaughters Janet Harren and Rachel Harren. His loom went to his grandson—perhaps his children already owned looms.

In his will, James shows his appreciation for her lifelong support: "I will and devise to my beloved wife, Martha, her bed and bed furniture her choice of my bay mares and her saddle, and her choice of two cows and six sheep & she to have the backroom of the house I now live in, and pasture on said plantation for her creatures aforementioned."

The plantation at that time was the one near Church Hill on the present Renninger Road and Oelig Road His sons John and Hance received other portions of this plantation and farm equipment. From these considerations, it appears that Martha had been a good and steadfast wife for those many years from 1745 to 1778. He also left to Martha some books previously mentioned: a large Bible, "whatsens body of divinity & Brouns Explanation of the Romons." There is no mention of his prior farms in Mt. Joy or Upton; one must assume he had disposed of them before.

McCullogh's descendants would carry on and thrive, writing the next chapter in the uniquely American experience. The family was born out of perhaps the most significant and intriguing era in Conococheague-area history. This diary presents many aspects that help us understand the issues that the early settlers faced in their new homeland on the Appalachian frontier. By careful examination of the cryptic entries in this diary, some of the puzzling of layers of history can be peeled away to expose the struggles for existence, first without conflict and then during the hostile raids that occurred during the French & Indian War. By uncovering the past as recorded firsthand by McCullogh in this diary, we can obtain a better glimpse of what life was like.

Bibliography/ References

Abbott, W. W. (ed). *The Papers of George Washington, Colonial Series.* Ten volume set covering 1748-1775. Charlottesville: University Press of Virginia 1983

Anderson, Fred. *The Crucible of War The Seven Years War and the Fate of Empire in British North America, 1754-1766.* New York: Vintage Press 2000 (reprint edition).

Anderson-Wolfe, Elizabeth B. *Early History and Genealogy of the Anderson-McCulllough- McCune Families and Related Lines of Franklin County, Pa.* No publisher or publishing date given. Out of print but available as a PDF at http://mccullohreunion.org/wp-content/uploads/2013/11/The-White-Book.pdf

Bolton, Charles Knowles, *Scotch Irish Pioneers in Ulster and America.* London: Forgotten Books, 2012.

Bricker, Calvin & Powell, Walter L. *Conflict on the Conococheague, 1755-1758: Terror in the Backcountry of Pennsylvania and Maryland.* Mercersburg, Pa.: The Conococheague Institute, 2009

Colloway, Colin G. *New Worlds for All: Indians, Europeans and the Remaking of Early America.* Baltimore, Md.: Johns Hopkins University Press, 1997

"Colonial Military Organization of Lower Path Valley." *Kittocht-inny Historical Society Papers, Vol. 15*. Chambersburg, Pa.: Kittochtinny Historical Society.

Conrad, William. *From Terror to Freedom in the Cumberland Valley*. Greencastle, Pa.: Lilian S. Besore Memorial Library, 1976.

Crytzer, Brady J. *Fort Pitt: A Frontier History*. Charleston, S.C.: The History Press, 2012.

Day, Sherman (ed.) *Historical Collections of the State of Pennsylvania*. Philadelphia: George W. Gorton, 1842. Reprint edition, Ulan Press, 2012

Dobson, David. *The Original Scots Colonists of Early America 1612-1783*. Baltimore, Md.: Genealogical Publishing Company, 1989

Donehoo, George Patterson. *A History of the Cumberland Valley in Pennsylvania*. Two volumes. Harrisburg, Pa.: Susquehanna History Association, 1930.

Dunaway, Wayland F. *Scotch-Irish of Colonial Pennsylvania. 1944*. Reprinted 1997. Baltimore: Genealogical Publishing Company.

Eschenmann, Hayes R. *The Three Mountain Road*. Shippensburg, Pa.: Published by the author, 2001.

Eschenmann, Hayes R. *Forbes Expedition, Cowan's Gap to Juniata Crossing*. Shippensburg, Pa.: Published by the author, 2003.

Fendrick, Virginia Shannon. *American Revolutionary Soldiers of Franklin County Pennsylvania*. Chambersburg: The Franklin County Chapter of Daughters of the American Revolution, 1969.

Forman, Harry E. "Surveying with Colonel Henry Bouquet." *Kittochtinny Historical Society Papers, Vol. 9*. Chambersburg, Pa.: Kittochtinny Historical Society, 1964

Heefner, Nancy, McCulloh, Joan, & Stenger, Betty (eds.). *The Tuscarora Reader,* Mercersburg Historical Society, 2000.

History of Franklin County, Pennsylvania: Containing a History of the County, Its Townships, Towns, Villages, Schools, Churches, Industries, Etc., Portraits of Early Settlers and Prominent Men, Biographies, History of Pennsylvania, Statistical and Miscellaneous Matter, Etc., Etc. Chicago: Warner, Beers & Company, 1887. Available online as part of PA's Past: Digital Bookshelf at Penn State.

Houpt, James. I*n His own Words: Diary of James McCullough.* Maitland, Fl.: Xulon Press, 2013

Hunter, William A. *Forts on the Pennsylvania Frontier 1753-1758.* Lewisburg, Pa.: Wennawoods Publishing, 1999

Ingles, Thomas. *The Story of Mary Draper Ingles and Son Thomas Ingles.* The original manuscript is the University of Virginia library in the Albert and Shirley Small Special Collection. It is very difficult to read, with little punctuation and poor spelling. It was later published as *Escape from Indian: The Story of Mary Draper Ingles and Thomas Ingles* by Roberta Ingles Steele and Andrew Lewis Ingles. Cambridge University Press, 1968

Jemison, Mary. *A Narrative of the Life of Mrs. Mary Jemison.* Project Gutenberg EBook, http://www.gutenberg.org/files/6960/6960-h/6960-h.htm

Jones, Henry Ford. *The Scotch-Irish in America.* Princeton: Princeton University Press, 1915.

Kraft, Herbert C. *The Lenape: Archeology, History, and Ethnology.* Newark: New Jersey Historical Society, 1986

Lacour, Harold. *Guide to Published Lists of Early Immigrants to North America, Third Edition*, 1938. Revised by Richard J. Wolfe. New York: New York Public Library, 1963.

Lowry, Jean. *A Journal of the Captivity of Jean Lowry and her Children.* Mercersburg, Pa.: Conococheague Institute, 2008.

Lucier, Armand. *Francis. French and Indian War Notices Abstracted from Colonial Newspapers, Vol. II, 1756-1757*. Westminster, Md.: Heritage Books, Inc., 2009.

McClure, C. Arnold. *A History Between the Rivers: The Susquehanna, the Juniata, and the Potomac, 1609-1959*. Xlibris Corp., 2009.

McCook, H. C. "Scotch Irish Women Pioneers," *Scotch-Irish Society of America Proceedings, Vol. VII*, 1897

McConnell, Michael N. *Country Between: The Upper Ohio Valley and its Peoples, 1724-1774*. Lincoln: University of Nebraska Press, 1992.

Merrill, James H. *Into the American Woods: Negotiators on the Pennsylvania Frontier*. New York: W.W. Norton and Company, 1999.

Miller, Kerby, Shreier, Arnold, Boling, Bruce and Doyle, David (eds.). *Irish Immigrants in the Land of Canaan*. New York: Oxford U. Press, 2003.

"Minutes of the Provincial Council of Pennsylvania," *Pennsylvania Colonial Records, Vol.s 1-16*.

Northrop, Henry Davenport. *Indian Horrors or Massacres by the Red Men.* 1899

Parkman, Francis. *Montcalm and Wolfe, Vols. 1 & 2*. Boston: Little Brown and Company, 1908.

Perceval-Maxwell, M. *Outbreak of the Irish Rebellion of 1641*. Kingston, Ont.: Queens University School of Policy, 1994.

Rupp, I. D. *Early History of Western Pennsylvania and of the West*, A.P. Ingram, 1848. Reprint edition, Lewisburg, Pa.: Wennawoods Publishing, 1995.

Ryan, James. *Irish Church Records: Their History, Availability and Use in Family & Local History Research. Second edition.* Dublin: Flyleaf Press, 2001.

Schaumanor, Marri Lou Schrionie. *Indictments, 1750-1800.* Cumberland County, Pennsylvania. Self-published, 1989.

Stoner, Charles J., " The Journal of James McCullough, An Historical Document," February 23, 1984. *Kittochittiny Historical Society Papers, Vol. 18*, pages 257-266.

Swanson, Neil. *Allegheny Uprising.* Rahway, N.J.: Quinn & Company, Inc., 1937.

Tax Records of Cumberland Valley, Peters, Antrim Townships 1750, 1751, 1753. Morri Lou Scribner Schaumann, 1974, Wollsville, Pa.

Tully, Alan. *William Penn's Legacy Politics and Social Structure in Provincial Pennsylvania 1726-1755.* Baltimore: John Hopkins University Press, 1977.

Turner, Frederick Jackson. *The Frontier in American History.* New York: Henry Holt and Company, 1920, 1947.

Virdin, Donald V. *Pennsylvania Genealogy and Family Histories.* Westminster, Md.: Heritage Books, Inc., 1992.

Waddell, Lois M. and Bomberger, Bruce D. *The French and Indian War in Pennsylvania 1753 -1763.* Harrisburg, Pennsylvania Historical and Museum Commission, 1996.

Watson, Thomas. *A Body of Divinity, 1692.* Carlisle, Pa.: Banner of Truth Trust, Revised edition, 1965, reprinted 1983.

Woodward, W.E. *A New American History.* New York: Garden City Publishing Co, Inc., 1936.

Women's Club of Mercersburg, Pennsylvania. *Old Mercersburg.* Published under the Auspices of the Journal of American History by Frank Allaben. New York: Genealogical Company, 1912. Nabu Press, 2010.

Acknowledgments

It is beyond our imagination to understand the reasons for these notations by James McCullogh and beyond our expectations that his descendants would treasure and safe keep it for future generations such as ours. After 200 years, the family kindly returned it to the place of its roots, Mercersburg, for continued safekeeping, then under the care of the historian Charles Stoner.

We need to thank the persons whose hands it is now in, Paula Stoner Reed, for kindly providing first copies of the text and then the booklet itself for making digital copies of each page for examination. This has made it possible to re-examine each page to take a better look at the writing and the context of the entries.

This analysis did not have to start from scratch, but had the benefit of prior interpretations.

One was the pioneering work of Charles Stoner who presented his findings in a talk to the Kittochtinny (Franklin Counry, PA) Historical Society February 23, 1984, and then prepared it for publication in the Kittochtinny Papers.

A very scholarly look at his diary was then published in 2003 in chapters 22 and 23 of *Irish Immigrants In the Land of Canaan*, chapters prepared by Kerby Miller.

Several of us from Conococheague Institute sat down to work together on a careful analysis of the text in the context of this locality in the western part of the Cumberland Valley, this region where James McCullogh settled in 1752. Each review of the text would bring to light new insight into the interpretations.

After some time one of our group, James W. Houpt, chose to take the knowledge that he had then and write it up from a fictionalized standpoint, which he published in 2013 under the title *In his Own Words The Diary of James McCullough 1722-1781 One Mans Chronicle of Colonial History.*

All of this prior work contributed to our desire to undertake as deep an analysis as would be possible to shed light on the book and its interpretation for present day understanding. James McCullogh encountered many challenges of a new farm on a wild frontier that deteriorated into a period of French and Indian War turbulence. We have visited many of the locations that McCullogh had mentioned, walked the paths, visited church sites and talked to many people who shared their knowledge. We owe our thanks to all who helped with this.

A considerable amount of archival work was carried out on the computer and in libraries for this work. We must thank Ann Allen for her extensive searches in efforts to establish family relationships and to determine who the parents and ancestors of James McCullogh were, researching the name in Pennsylvania, Virginia, North Carolina and North Ireland. James Houpt gratefully shared his information including contacts with genealogy sources in Northern Ireland, as well as many other aspects of interpretation of the entries. We thank the staffs of these and other libraries for their assistance, especially the Kittochtinny in Chambersburg, the Cumberland County Library in Carlisle, the Adams County Library in Gettysburg, and the Western Maryland Room of the Washington County Free Library in Hagerstown, Md.

Members of the Conococheague Institute community provided regular review and support of the work in progress including Gay Buchanan, our longtime dependable supporter, Leda Werner as secretary, Joan McKean, our librarian, who also prepared the index for this book, John Munday, our genealogist Board member, the historian Roger Swartz, Cindy Fink, as well as staff and volunteers. This was time-consuming work. With the extensive attention given to this work it is hoped that errors of reading the text and interpretative errors have been reduced to a minimum. As the interpretation was unable to be precise, we must caution the reader that while we have done our best, additional details could come to light in the future.

APPENDIX 1

Brief Summary of James McCullogh's Travels

Immigration Steps

Many McCulloghs left the lowlands of the southern Scottish coast and Cardonnes Castle at Firth on Forth and crossed the north Irish Sea to Northern Ireland in the 1600's. Travel across these waters was easy and many Scots then lived in Northern Ireland for decades.

Emigration from Ireland resulted from political changes that made life difficult and they become convinced that the British government had mistreated them. Numerous McCulloghs migrated from Northern Ireland to North America in the first part of the eighteenth cntury, with many coming to Pennsylvania, but some to Maryland and North Carolina. Archibald McCullogh, an older brother of James came about 1740. The trip across the Atlantic in crowded boats took a matter of months, with many dying of disease and poor nutrition.

James McCullogh bought his passage in 1745, but seems to have crossed the Atlantic in early 1746 disembarking at Newcastle, De.

In 1747, he became joint owner of land in Mt Joy Township now Adams County in the Marsh Creek settlement area south of present Gettysburg. There his diary records farming operations for several years and linen making. He and Josiah Simpson had purchased 200 acres from Robert Horner. Adams County had many more Scotch-Irish than any other ethnic group.

In September 1752, he bought a new farm at a sheriff's sale 40 miles further west over the Blue Ridge Mountains in the Cumberland Valley in the Conococheague settlement near the west branch of this creek. South of present Upton and west of Greencastle, it was then in Peters and now Montgomery township. In 1753 he was building infrastructure and getting settled on this new farm.

Sometime between 1757 and 1764 he again moved to a new farm, this time only about five mile away near Church Hill, four miles east of present Mercersburg and near the Presbyterian Church that he attended. He remained here until he died in 1781.

Trips from the Frontier for Safety

During the time of dangers from Indian attacks during the French and Indian War period, these trips are recorded:

July 12, 1755 "was put to flight by a fals alarm from ye Ingens". Probably only brief.

"was put to flight by a report of ye Indins agust ye 6th".

"ye great cove was burnt Noveber ye first & our flight to Mash Creek was Novr ye 2 1755". Returned February 1756.

For this 40 mile trip each way he had to take his wife, Martha, and children, Jean, John, James, and Mary. The distance to Antietam would have been much easier a distance of 20-25 miles with no mountain to cross.

When he fled to the Antietam settlement;,who he stayed with is not known but there seems to have been an Alexander McCullogh in the region. He returned late spring with family staying at a house on the great road near Cross's Fort, a safe house 5 miles south near the main branch of the Conococheague Creek.

Sons, John and James, were taken captive from his Upton farm on July 26 1756.

After several years, on advice of a trader from Shippensburg, James made an excursion and negotiated release of his son, John, from the Indians but son John refused because he had forgotten the English language, and escaped from his father at night to return to the Indians.

In spite of the sorrow this must have had on James and his other family members, he does not make the slightest indication in his diary, leaving us the guess time and the year when he made the trip, a distance of 200 miles or so.

APPENDIX 2

Petition of McColoch (McCullough)
[B.M., Add. MSS. 21655.f. 112.D.S.]

Whereas John McCulloh ¹ aged thirteen Years, Brown Complex-ion, and a Brown or Mousemark on his right knee — James McCulloh Aged ten years, fair Complexion with a large Mold on his right Groin; Were carried away from their Father James McCulloh in the Month of Augst 1756 from his Plantation near Fort Loudon, by the indians, when he the said James and the rest of his Family narrowly escaped the fate of his Wretched Children.

The eldest Boy is Said to be kept by a Deleware Indian near the Salt Licks, ² and the other was given up to a French Ensign then at Fort Du Quesne, but what became of him Since he knows not. ³

The loss of the above Boys make their unhappy Parents truly wretched, therefore Recommend their distressed case to all Charitable and well disposed Christians.

NB. The Said James McCulloh (notwithstanding his low Circum-stances) is willing to give any reward in his power for bringing in the above Children. ⁴

Fort Pitt the 3rd of June 1761 — [Endorsed by Bouquet]

Description of McCulloch Children Prisoners among Indians.

[1] Many years later, apparently in 1806, John McCullough wrote an account of his captivity among the Delawares from 1756 to 1764, which is in MG-6, Pa. State Archives, Harrisburg, Pa. It is printed as "A Narrative of the Captivity of John McCullogh, Esq. Written by Himself," in Archibald Loudon, ed., A Selection of Some of the Most Interesting Narratives of Outrages, Committed by the Indians, in Their Wars, with White People, 2 vols (1808-1811; reprint ed., New York, 1971, 252-301.

[2] This information had been brought to James McCullough, the father, by Andrew Wilkins, an Indian trader who had seen John at Salt Licks (present-day Niles, Ohio). Account of John McCullough [1806], MG-6, Pa. State Arch.

[3] Evidently he was never found.

4 James McCullough visited his son John early in 1761 hoping to return him to white society. He failed but in 1762, much against his son's wishes, he traveled to Venango and bought him from John's Indian "brother." John escaped, returned to the Delawares, and lived with them until Pontiac's War. Late in 1764, apparently voluntarily, he returned to his parents. Account of John McCullough [1806], MG-6, Pa. State Arch.

From *The Papers of Henry Bouquet, Volume V, September 1, 1760-October 31, 1761*, published by The Pennsylvania Historical and Museum Commission (Harrisburg, 1984).

Index